Sea Breezes at The Beach House Hotel

by

Judith Keim

NOVELS BY JUDITH KEIM

THE HARTWELL WOMEN SERIES:
    The Talking Tree – 1
    Sweet Talk – 2
    Straight Talk – 3
    Baby Talk – 4
    The Hartwell Women – Boxed Set

THE BEACH HOUSE HOTEL SERIES:
    Breakfast at The Beach House Hotel – 1
    Lunch at The Beach House Hotel – 2
    Dinner at The Beach House Hotel – 3
    Christmas at The Beach House Hotel – 4
    Margaritas at The Beach House Hotel – 5
    Dessert at The Beach House Hotel – 6
    Coffee at The Beach House Hotel – 7
    High Tea at The Beach House Hotel – 8
    Nightcaps at The Beach House Hotel – 9
    Bubbles at The Beach House Hotel – 10
    Canapes at The Beach House Hotel – 11
    Sea Breezes at The Beach House Hotel – 12

THE FAT FRIDAYS GROUP:
    Fat Fridays – 1
    Sassy Saturdays – 2
    Secret Sundays – 3

THE SALTY KEY INN SERIES:
    Finding Me – 1
    Finding My Way – 2
    Finding Love – 3
    Finding Family – 4
    The Salty Key Inn Series – Boxed Set

SEASHELL COTTAGE BOOKS:
    A Christmas Star
    Change of Heart
    A Summer of Surprises
    A Road Trip to Remember
    The Beach Babes

THE CHANDLER HILL INN SERIES:
    Going Home – 1
    Coming Home – 2
    Home at Last – 3
    The Chandler Hill Inn Series – Boxed Set

THE DESERT SAGE INN SERIES:
    The Desert Flowers – Rose – 1
    The Desert Flowers – Lily – 2
    The Desert Flowers – Willow – 3
    The Desert Flowers – Mistletoe & Holly – 4
    The Desert Sage Inn Series – Boxed Set

SOUL SISTERS AT CEDAR MOUNTAIN LODGE:
    Christmas Sisters – Anthology
    Christmas Kisses
    Christmas Castles
    Christmas Stories – Soul Sisters Anthology
    Christmas Joy
    The Christmas Joy Boxed Set

THE SANDERLING COVE INN SERIES:
    Waves of Hope – 1
    Sandy Wishes – 2
    Salty Kisses – 3

THE LILAC LAKE INN SERIES
    Love by Design – 1
    Love Between the Lines – 2
    Love Under the Stars – 3

LILAC LAKE BOOKS
- Love's Cure
- Love's Home Run
- Love's Bloom
- Love's Harvest
- Love's Match

OTHER BOOKS:
- The ABCs of Living With a Dachshund
- Trouble At The Winston Hotel... A Mouse Mystery
- Holiday Hopes
- The Winning Tickets

For more information: **www.judithkeim.com**

PRAISE FOR JUDITH KEIM'S NOVELS

THE BEACH HOUSE HOTEL SERIES – Books 1 – 12:
"Love the characters in this series. This series was my first introduction to Judith Keim. She is now one of my favorites. Looking forward to reading more of her books."

<u>BREAKFAST AT THE BEACH HOUSE HOTEL</u> – "An easy, delightful read that offers romance, family relationships, and strong women learning to be stronger. Real life situations filter through the pages. Enjoy!"

<u>LUNCH AT THE BEACH HOUSE HOTEL</u> – "This series is such a joy to read. You feel you are actually living with them. Can't wait to read the latest one."

<u>DINNER AT THE BEACH HOUSE HOTEL</u> – "A Terrific Read! As usual, Judith Keim did it again. Enjoyed immensely. Continue writing such pleasantly reading books for all of us readers."

<u>CHRISTMAS AT THE BEACH HOUSE HOTEL</u> – "Not Just Another Christmas Novel. This is book number four in the series and my introduction to Judith Keim's writing. I wasn't disappointed. The characters are dimensional and engaging. The plot is well crafted and advances at a pleasing pace.

<u>MARGARITAS AT THE BEACH HOUSE HOTEL</u> – "Overall, Margaritas at the Beach House Hotel is another wonderful addition to the series. Judith Keim takes the reader on a journey told through the voices of these amazing characters we have all come to love through the years!

<u>DESSERT AT THE BEACH HOUSE HOTEL</u> – "It is a heartwarming and beautiful women's fiction as only Judith Keim can do with her wonderful characters,

amazing location. and family and friends whose daily lives circle around Ann and Rhonda and The Beach House Hotel.

<u>COFFEE AT THE BEACH HOUSE HOTEL</u> – "Great story and characters! A hard to put down book. Lots of things happening, including a kidnapping of a young boy. The beach house hotel is a wonderful hotel run by two women who are best friends. Highly recommend this book.

<u>HIGH TEA AT THE BEACH HOUSE HOTEL</u> – "What a lovely story! The Beach House Hotel series is always a great read. Each book in the series brings a new aspect to the saga of Ann and Rhonda."

THE HARTWELL WOMEN SERIES – Books 1 – 4:
"This was an EXCELLENT series. When I discovered Judith Keim, I read all of her books back to back. I thoroughly enjoyed the women Keim has written about. They are believable and you want to just jump into their lives and be their friends! I can't wait for any upcoming books!"

"I fell into Judith Keim's Hartwell Women series and have read & enjoyed all of her books in every series. Each centers around a strong & interesting woman character and their family interaction. Good reads that leave you wanting more."

THE FAT FRIDAYS GROUP – Books 1 – 3:
"Excellent story line for each character, and an insightful representation of situations which deal with some of the contemporary issues women are faced with today."

THE SALTY KEY INN SERIES – Books 1 – 4:
FINDING ME – "The characters are endearing with the same struggles we all encounter. The setting makes me feel like I am a guest at The Salty Key Inn…relaxed, happy

& light-hearted! The men are yummy and the women strong. You can't get better than that! Happy Reading!"

FINDING MY WAY- "Loved the family dynamics as well as uncertain emotions of dating and falling in love. Appreciated the morals and strength of parenting throughout. Just couldn't put this book down."

FINDING LOVE – "Judith Keim always puts substance into her books. This book was no different, I learned about PTSD, accepting oneself, there are always going to be problems but stick it out and make it work.

FINDING FAMILY – "Completing this series is like eating the last chip. Love Judith's writing and her female characters are always smart, strong, vulnerable to life and love experiences."

"This was a refreshing book. Bringing the heart and soul of the family to us."

THE CHANDLER HILL INN SERIES – Books 1 – 3:

GOING HOME – "I was completely immersed in this book, with the beautiful descriptive writing, and the author's way of bringing her characters to life. I felt like I was right inside her story."

COMING HOME – "Coming Home was such a wonderful story. The author has such a gift for getting the reader right to the heart of things."

HOME AT LAST – "In this wonderful conclusion, to a heartfelt and emotional trilogy set in Oregon's stunning wine country, Judith Keim has tied up the Chandler Hill series with the perfect bow."

SEASHELL COTTAGE BOOKS:

A CHRISTMAS STAR – "Love, laughter, sadness, great food, and hope for the future, all in one book. It doesn't get any better than this stunning read."

CHANGE OF HEART – "CHANGE OF HEART is the summer read we've all been waiting for. Judith Keim is a master at creating fascinating characters that are simply irresistible. Her stories leave you with a big smile on your face and a heart bursting with love."

~Kellie Coates Gilbert, author of the popular Sun Valley Series

A SUMMER OF SURPRISES – "Ms. Keim uses this book as an amazing platform to show that with hard emotional work, belief in yourself, and love, the scars of abuse can be conquered. It in no way preaches, it's a lovely story with a happy ending."

A ROAD TRIP TO REMEMBER – "The characters are so real that they jump off the page. Such a fun, HAPPY book at the perfect time. It will lift your spirits and even remind you of your own grandmother. Spirited and hopeful Aggie gets a second chance at love and she takes the steering wheel and drives straight for it."

THE BEACH BABES – "Another winner at the pen of Judith Keim. I love the characters and the book just flows. It feels as though you are at the beach with them and are a part of you.

THE DESERT SAGE INN SERIES – Books 1 – 4:
THE DESERT FLOWERS – ROSE – "The Desert Flowers - Rose, "In this first of a series, we see each woman come into her own and view new beginnings even as they must take this tearful journey as they slowly lose a dear friend.

THE DESERT FLOWERS – LILY – "The second book in the Desert Flowers series is just as wonderful as the first. Judith Keim is a brilliant storyteller. Her characters are truly lovely and people that you want to be friends with as soon as you start reading. Judith Keim is not afraid to weave real-life conflict and loss into her stories.

THE DESERT FLOWERS – WILLOW – "The feelings of love, joy, happiness, friendship, family, and the pain of loss are deeply felt by Willow Sanchez and her two cohorts Rose and Lily. The Desert Flowers met because of their deep feelings for Alec Thurston, a man who touched their lives in different ways."

MISTLETOE AND HOLLY – "As always, the author never ceases to amaze me. She's able to take characters and bring them to life in such a way that you think you're actually among family. It's a great holiday read. You won't be disappointed."

THE SANDERLING COVE INN SERIES

WAVES OF HOPE – "Such a wonderful story about several families in a beautiful location in Florida. A grandmother requests her three granddaughters to help her by running the family's inn for the summer. Other grandmothers in the area played a part in this plan to find happiness for their grandsons and granddaughters."

SANDY WISHES – "Three cousins needing a change and a few of the neighborhood boys from when they were young are back visiting their grandmothers. It is an adventure, a summer of discoveries, and embracing the person they are becoming."

SALTY KISSES – "I love this story, as well as the entire series because it's about family, friendship, and love. The meddling grandmothers have only the best intentions and want to see their grandchildren find love and happiness. What grandparent wouldn't want that?"

THE LILAC LAKE INN SERIES – Books 1 – 3:

LOVE BY DESIGN – "Genie Wittner is planning on selling

her beloved Lilac Inn B&B, and keeping a cottage for her three granddaughters, Whitney, the movie star, Dani an architect, and Taylor a writer. A little mystery, a possible ghost, and romance all make this a great read and the start of a new series."

LOVE BETWEEN THE LINES – "Taylor is one of 3 sisters who have inherited a cottage in Lilac Lake from their grandmother. She is an accomplished author who is having some issues getting inspired for her next book. Things only get worse when she receives an email from her new editor with a harsh critique of her last book. She's still fuming when Cooper shows up in town, determined to work together on getting the book ready."

LOVE UNDER THE STARS – "Love Under the Stars is the third book in The Lilac Lake Inn Series by author Judith Keim. Judith beautifully weaves together the final story in this amazing series about the Gilford sisters and their grandmother, GG."

THE LILAC LAKE BOOKS

LOVE'S CURE – Welcome back to Lilac Lake with a new spin-off series from author Judith Keim. For fans of the author, you will be reunited with previous characters, as well as being introduced to new ones.

Sea Breezes at The Beach House Hotel

The Beach House Hotel Series – Book 12

by
Judith Keim

Wild Quail Publishing

Sea Breezes at The Beach House Hotel is a work of fiction. Names, characters, places, public or private institutions, corporations, towns, and incidents are the product of the author's imagination or are used fictitiously. Any resemblance to actual events, locales, or persons, living or dead, is coincidental.

No part of *Sea Breezes at The Beach House Hotel* may be reproduced or transmitted in any form or by any electronic or mechanical means, including information storage and retrieval systems, without permission in writing from the author, except by a reviewer who may quote brief passages in a review. This book may not be resold or uploaded for distribution to others. For permissions, contact the author directly via electronic mail:

wildquail.pub@gmail.com
www.judithkeim.com

Published in the United States of America by:

Wild Quail Publishing
PO Box 171332
Boise, ID 83717-1332

ISBN# 978-1-965622-43-8
Copyright ©2026, Judith Keim
All rights reserved

Dedication

Dedicated with love to my husband, Peter, who's always loved sailing.

CHAPTER ONE

ONE BRIGHT, SUNNY MORNING IN LATE NOVEMBER, I sat with my best friend and business partner, Rhonda Grayson, in our office at The Beach House Hotel on Florida's Gulf Coast. We were going over preparations for the holidays. Thanksgiving was a big event for guests and locals alike. Early on the morning of the day after Thanksgiving, the hotel would be transformed with Christmas holiday decorations everywhere on the property. "High Season" lasted from that time until Easter, and we, along with our staff, were caught up in a whirlwind as we ran the hotel.

My cell phone rang, and I eagerly answered it. *Vaughn's daughter, Nell.*

"Hi, Darling. How are you? I can't wait until you and Clint and the kids get here for Thanksgiving."

I listened to her, growing increasingly concerned as she explained she would be driving alone with her two children. Due to an important business deal, Clint would fly in on Thanksgiving and leave the next day

"Oh, I'm sorry to hear that," I said. "Your father will be disappointed that he and Clint won't have time for sailing."

Nell spoke to me in a flurry of angry words and then stopped, letting out a tortured sigh. "I really need to talk to you, Ann. Will you promise me some moments alone?"

"Of course. I hate to hear you sounding so unhappy."

"It'll be great to be in Sabal with you and Dad," Nell said. "I'd better go. I'll let you know when I get close to town."

We ended the call. I sat staring into space, feeling uneasy.

"Is Nell okay?" Rhonda asked me. She loved Nell.

"She and the kids are traveling to Florida this weekend for Thanksgiving week. I'm thrilled they're coming, but I'm worried about her. She seemed depressed, even angry."

Rhonda gave me a sympathetic look. "Aw, Annie, all she needs is to get away from D.C. and enjoy some of our sea breezes. That will help straighten out her life."

"I hope you're right because it's unlike Nell to be so down. I'm sure it has something to do with Clint, but I didn't want to have that kind of discussion with her over the phone. She wants some privacy with me when she gets here."

"She's always wanted her family to move to Sabal. It would be much easier for everyone to be together. She and Liz are close, too, which would make it nice for both of them," said Rhonda.

"Right now, I need to concentrate on being supportive." I shook my head. "I have a bad feeling about this."

Rhonda said. "I'm sorry. How about taking a stroll with me on the beach? I could use a break."

Walking on the beach was a way for Rhonda and me to talk in private, as long as we didn't run into our neighbor, Brock Goodwin, the president of the Neighborhood Association.

We left the office, and I breathed in the salty tang of the air. It was a cool, late November morning. At this time of year, weather changes were to be expected, but I knew the day would soon warm to a very pleasant temperature.

We took off our shoes and stepped onto the sand.

Standing near the lacy edge of the water, I lifted my face to the sun, loving the gentle sea breeze that caressed my cheeks. The sound of the waves meeting the shore and pulling away helped me to relax. That soothing movement was as old as time, but it always worked for me. Seagulls and terns above us swirled in the wind, their cries telling a story of their own.

"Whenever I stand back and look at our hotel, I can't believe we own it," said Rhonda, throwing her arm across my shoulder. Lying next to the shore, The Beach House Hotel resembled a lazy Roseate Spoonbill with its pink surface and sweet curves.

I smiled at her. "We've both worked hard at making it succeed."

"A lot of people didn't believe we could do it," said Rhonda. "But we'll keep going until our daughters take over for us."

"With Angela and Liz raising our grandchildren, it won't happen very soon. But the thought is tantalizing."

"Who would've thunk we'd be this successful?" said Rhonda, grinning at me.

"It certainly hasn't been a breeze, but all the work has been worth it. Especially because it's been you and me as a team from the beginning."

"You know, Annie, I knew we'd be a match because we're very different," said Rhonda.

"I'll say." After my parents were killed in an automobile accident, I was raised in Boston by a strict grandmother, who would be appalled by the changes in my life. Rhonda grew up in a loving family in a tough neighborhood in New Jersey. Though I'd gotten used to Rhonda's colorful language, it still sometimes surprised me.

"Do you remember how you told me not to be so beige when we first met?" I asked her.

"Aw-w-w, you know I just wanted to help you make some changes after your divorce," Rhonda said. "I knew I could never be as classy as you, but I could show you a fun time."

We laughed together. Rhonda was my best friend, and I loved her.

We strolled along the sand, talking about the high teas we were planning for our high season. We'd started offering them after a guest had demanded them, and now they were part of our winter season festivities.

I stared down at the footprints that sanderlings and sandpipers had left behind in the sand at the edge of the water. I loved the little signs that they'd been there.

Rhonda nudged me and hissed, "Oh no! Here he comes."

Lifting my head, I stared at Brock Goodwin, surprised to see him here at this time of day. It was too late to try to move away. We were stuck.

"Hello, ladies," said Brock, hurrying up to us. "You're just the people I needed to see. My import business has just received a supply of spectacular fireworks for New Year's Eve celebrations, along with a variety of Christmas decorations. I can offer you a discount on them if you place your order right away. They're going fast."

As enticing as it sounded, Rhonda and I looked at each other and shook our heads.

"Thanks, but no thanks," I said.

"Hotels and condo buildings up and down the beach have ordered some," said Brock. "Afraid you can't compete?"

"As you surely learned from the Italian restaurant business you were associated with, we don't have to compete," said Rhonda.

"So, I made a mistake," said Brock, trying to shrug it off as the truth trapped him. He'd lost money helping a chef attempt to hurt our business.

"More than one mistake," said Rhonda. "See ya later."

Brock stood breathing heavily with frustration, and then he turned and walked away, his feet childishly pounding the sand.

"It's a nice idea to have fireworks," I said. "Too bad we can't trust him."

"I'll never be able to trust him," said Rhonda. "He's a total jackass. Besides, there are all those liability issues with setting off fireworks."

"True. We don't need those expenses."

We stood facing one another. Our morning walk was ruined. Brock always wanted to find a way to harm us and our business.

That evening, I spoke to Vaughn about my concerns with Nell. "It's not like her to be depressed and out of sorts. I can't wait for her to come here, where I can really talk to her as she wants."

"I'm grateful you and she have a close relationship," said Vaughn, handing me a glass of red wine as we sat on the lanai. "I don't like it when our children are having problems."

"She and Clint have been married for over ten years now. Maybe they need to revive their relationship. With their visit, perhaps we can offer to have the kids stay here with us while Nell and Clint go off by themselves."

"I'll be home for a while and should be able to help with that," said Vaughn. "Let's wait and see what the situation is before we make plans. Nell will be here in a couple of days. On a brighter note, I heard from Nicholas Swain. He's going to send me a script to look at for a movie he's working on. He and Tina are coming to The Beach House Hotel for Christmas. He wants me to take him sailing."

"Oh, how nice. I didn't notice their name on the reservations list. But I'm thrilled they'll be here." Tina Marks was a young movie star whom Rhonda and I helped soon after we opened the hotel. She'd become like a daughter to us.

"Nicholas said they'd reserved a guesthouse under a different name," said Vaughn. "After the kidnapping incident with their son, they don't travel anywhere unless it's under an assumed name for protection."

"That makes sense," I said, remembering how Rhonda

and I had been involved in saving her son.

My cell phone chimed. *Tina Marks.*

"Hi," I said cheerfully. "Vaughn and I were just discussing you and Nicholas. I understand you will be here at the hotel for the Christmas holidays. I can't wait to see you."

We chatted for several minutes and then Tina said, "With both boys in school, I'm finding myself with some extra time. I'm hoping to come more often to Florida to be with you and Rhonda."

"We'd love it. Better watch out or we'll put you to work," I teased.

"Sounds terrific. I haven't found a new movie role that interests me. Besides, at my age, it's hard to find appropriate ones," Tina said.

"Your age? You're not even forty," I said.

"Pretty close. That's what I mean," Tina said. "Gotta go. See you in a few weeks."

I ended the call and turned to Vaughn. "Tina says she's having difficulty finding movie roles because of her age. It's very unfair, Men supposedly age gracefully, but women have to look as if they're in their twenties or early thirties to find work."

"That's true enough to be a problem," admitted Vaughn. "Hopefully, that will change. Tina is a very talented actress."

"Her mother got her started in movies when she was a young teen and put her in situations where she was taken advantage of and sexually abused to get parts in films for her."

"It's a creepy business for both men and women," said Vaughn, pulling me onto his lap. "I'd always give you a part in any film I was making."

I melted into his kiss and then pulled away. "It would have to be a juicy role, or I'd turn it down."

Vaughn and I laughed together.

The next day, I told Rhonda about my call with Tina. "I've been thinking we ought to take advantage of having Tina stay with us. Perhaps we could ask her to participate in our annual cancer fund-raising luncheon. Or something like that."

"It sounds like Tina needs to do something rewarding. It's hard for some mothers when all their children leave the toddler age and start elementary school. Maybe that's what's bothering Nell."

"Could be. We'll find out," I said, looking up as Bernie knocked on the door and entered.

Bernhard Bruner was our general manager, and we loved him. In the years since he'd been with us, he'd changed from a very regimented man to a more open person used to us and our routines.

"Hi, Bernie," said Rhonda. "What's up?"

"I just wanted your agreement on a matter. Brock Goodwin tried to sell me fireworks, and I turned him down. I figured after the last debacle with him, you'd want nothing to do with it."

"Absolutely correct," I said. "He approached us on the beach, and we told him no."

"Bernie, what will it take for us to get rid of him?" Rhonda asked.

He shrugged. "I can think of ways to do it. None of them legal." I burst into unexpected laughter. Bernie really was loosening up.

After he left, Rhonda and I shared another laugh about Bernie, and then I answered my cell. *Nell's husband, Clint.*

"Hi, Clint. How are you? We're thrilled Nell and the kids are coming early for Thanksgiving. I hope you'll be able to join them before the big day and stay a while."

"Hi, Ann. Thanks, I'd love to, but I can't do it. Unfortunately, I'm working on a big business deal. I hope I can persuade you to talk with Nell. She told me she's considering taking the kids out of school and staying in Florida throughout the holidays," said Clint. "That's not what we discussed. I hope you'll make her understand I have no choice but to try and close the deal."

I drew a deep breath to stop from saying something I might regret. "I'll do you the favor of listening to both of you. There are two sides to any story."

"Fair enough," said Clint. "I need to do this. It's part of my new job."

"Oh," I said, remembering how Clint and Nell had argued about the opportunity Clint was offered. Nell hadn't wanted him to take it.

"I've got to go. " I'm due to participate in an important meeting," Clint said. "Thank you, Ann. I appreciate your help."

He ended the call before I could clarify once again that I was willing to listen to each of them. That's all.

Rhonda looked at me. "Let me guess. Clint wants your help with Nell."

"He doesn't understand that I'm not going to solve any problems for him. That has to come from Nell and him."

"I remember how I disliked Angela's Reggie in the beginning," said Rhonda. "But as you once told me, I needed to trust her. I'd guess that's the kind of situation you'll find yourself in. Trust Nell to do the right thing."

"It's a worry," I said. "But as Vaughn says, we'll have to see how it all plays out."

Rhonda's cell rang. She picked up the call and listened, her expression becoming alarmed. "Oh, no! I'm sorry, honey. Annie and I will take care of things at the hotel for Lorraine. Tell her not to worry. And please give my condolences to Reggie."

Rhonda ended the call and turned to me in tears. "Arthur has died. I knew he wasn't in good health, but this was unexpected."

I got up out of my chair and hugged her. "I'm sorry. I had no idea he was so sick."

"I think Lorraine has been more worried about him than she has let on," said Rhonda. "I'll send her a text that we're here for her. But I'll wait until the situation has settled down this evening before I go visit her. Angie said that everyone is in shock because he seemed to be getting better."

I couldn't help the sting of tears. "It's such a shame. Lorraine and Arthur have been married for only a few years. Thank goodness, they were happy ones."

"This has been an upsetting day," said Rhonda, standing. "Let's go to our special hiding place and think about how we'll do without Lorraine for a while."

"Okay. I agree we need some time."

We headed for the lobby bar and the staircase behind it.

As we entered the bar, the bartender called out to us, "What can I get you?"

Rhonda and I exchanged a glance. "Should we?" I asked.

"Absolutely," Rhonda answered, then said to the bartender. "Will you make us something light and tasty?"

"How about a Seabreeze? Grapefruit juice, cranberry juice, and vodka."

"Perfect," Rhonda said. "Make sure we get a slice of lime. We need all the fruit we can get."

He laughed. "For you two, anything."

Moments later, Rhonda and I carried our drinks up to the doorway on the second floor that opened into a small storage area and a balcony beyond.

We took seats in the two chairs we kept there and looked out over the hotel property to the water beyond.

Rhonda held her glass high. "Here's to Arthur Smythe. May his soul rest in peace." I lifted my glass. "Amen."

A gentle breeze whirled around us.

CHAPTER TWO

THE NEXT COUPLE OF DAYS WERE HECTIC AS RHONDA AND I stepped in to help wherever we could at the hotel and did what was needed to support Angela and Reggie in dealing with the emotions and practical details following a death in the family.

On the Saturday before Thanksgiving, the same day as Nell was due to arrive with her children, I was assigned to help with a wedding. Nell promised to call me when she was about to enter Sabal, so I could race home to meet her. The guestrooms were ready for her and the children, with welcome gifts in each one.

The day was full of mixed emotions as I dealt with sadness over Arthur's passing, happiness for the wedding couple, and excitement for Nell's arrival. I arrived at the hotel to make sure the bridal party of six had a breakfast buffet before heading out to a morning at the spa and then a bride's luncheon at André's. The bride, Melinda Peterson, a sweet girl from Cohasset, Massachusetts, greeted me with a hug of enthusiasm. "Thank you, Ms. Sanders. Everything has been delightful. Henry and his parents agree."

"I'm delighted you're pleased. You have a beautiful day ahead of you. The garden looks lovely. It'll be a perfect setting for your wedding. Please let us know if you need anything."

"Thank you," she said, and I breathed a sigh of relief. Most weddings weren't this easy.

I went to check on the work status in the hospitality office. Lauren, who was now a co-wedding planner, was there reviewing her Excel spreadsheet.

"How is everything?" I asked her.

"Very well," she replied. "I've told Lorraine we have no worries, that she should just concentrate on her family." Her eyes filled with tears. "It's sad this has happened. Lorraine and Arthur were very happy together."

I swallowed hard. "It doesn't seem fair, I know. We'll have to be a big support to Lorraine in the coming weeks."

"Annette and I have already promised to take the lead on all social activities," said Lauren.

"Thank you. Rhonda and I appreciate all you're doing," I said. "You'll make sure the side lawn is set up well in advance of the ceremony today?"

"Oh, yes. Don't worry. I know your daughter is arriving today, and you want to be able to be with her."

"I'm hoping she gets here before noon, as she said. It's a lovely day for a wedding and a homecoming."

Though I continued doing work around the hotel, my mind stayed focused on Nell's arrival. We usually saw Nell and her family at least once or twice a year. I was eager to see how much the kids had grown. At eight, Bailey was the same age as Angela's Sally Kate. They loved to play together. Ned, at five, was about the same age as the triplets, and he and Noah were best buddies. It seemed a shame Nell's family had chosen to live and work in Washington, D.C., when the rest of the family wanted them to move to Sabal.

I was talking to the kitchen staff about the breakfast buffet for wedding guests tomorrow when my cell chimed with a call from Nell.

"We're almost there," said Nell, her voice sounding a lot more upbeat.

"Okay, I'm heading home from the hotel. I'll meet you there." I ended the call, phoned Lauren to give her the news, and left the hotel.

###

At home, Vaughn and I stood together in the driveway, our arms around each other as our black and tan dachshund, Cindy, gamboled at our feet, sensing our anticipation.

When Nell drove into the driveway, I raced forward to greet her as she got out of the car.

The kids climbed out of the back seat and went to Vaughn while I hung onto Nell. The worry I'd held since her call flared inside me as I studied the circles beneath her eyes and the lackluster smile she gave me.

"I'm overjoyed to see you," I said, hugging her tight. "You can relax in our warm sunshine."

"I'm looking forward to it," she said.

She stepped away and said, "Hi, Daddy," in a voice that reminded me of Liz when she was hurting.

I turned to Bailey and Ned, giving them my attention with hugs and kisses, then said, "C'mon. Let's get you inside. Then I bet you're ready for a swim in the pool."

"Hooray," said Ned, and I loved his enthusiasm.

Robbie emerged from the house and smiling at Nell said, "Hi, sis."

Nell stepped back and studied him. "You're grown even more since I last saw you. You're going to be as tall as Dad."

She gave him a hug. "Ned has been talking about his uncle."

"I want to go in the pool with you. I'm really fast," said Ned.

Robbie ruffled Ned's blond hair. "Glad to hear it."

He put his arm around Bailey, who gave Robbie an adoring smile. There was no doubt that she was going to be a beauty when she grew older. With butterscotch hair and big hazel eyes, she loved dressing up and was already very stylish.

"Was the drive difficult?" I asked Nell as I took her arm and led her inside.

"Not too bad. But I'm glad we decided to spend the night in Georgia. And the kids knew I needed them to behave, which is why they might get cranky later on."

"No worries. We're just happy you're all here. You can relax before the holiday."

"Before Clint comes," Nell said. "I really need to talk to you."

"I'm ready anytime, but I suggest we wait until tomorrow. The wedding will be over and you hopefully would have been able to get some sleep."

"I look like hell, don't I?" said Nell. "That's another thing I'm hoping for—some spa treatments and to get my hair cut and colored."

"No problem. After you get settled, we'll make those appointments. It's a busy season of year, but I can manage it."

Nell leaned her head against my shoulder. "That will be wonderful."

When we entered her guestroom, Nell saw the envelope I'd placed on her bed and smiled at me. "What delightful thing have you done for me?"

I laughed. I always treated Nell to something whenever she came for a visit.

Nell swept the envelope up into her hands and opened it. Grinning, she said, "Thank you. I need a new outfit, and Christine at *Styles* always knows what I like."

We hugged and I said, "I hope this stay will be healing for you."

Nell frowned. 'Me, too."

I left her to check on the kids. Bailey loved her sundress I'd left on her bed, and Ned held onto the bulldozer toy I'd bought him to use at the beach.

I helped get their clothing settled in their rooms while they went swimming with Robbie and Vaughn. As I filled their chests of drawers, I realized they'd each brought a lot of clothes. Were they prepared to spend the next few weeks here in Sabal instead of going home? It was something Nell and I would, no doubt, talk about.

I went to my room to change to go to the hotel. Rhonda and I tried to attend as many weddings as possible, and we always made an effort to dress for them. With Rhonda busy with her family, I would represent us.

I'd just slipped on my chocolate brown linen sheath when Nell appeared. "Liz told me about Arthur Smythe's death. I'm sorry. I want to go to the funeral service with her. Can we arrange for a sitter?"

"Yes, Liana will be glad to help, I'm sure. Vaughn and I pay her fees at the local community college in return for her babysitting when we need her. It works out well for both of us."

"I wish I had that arrangement at home," said Nell. "Though my social life is about zero,"

I studied her. "That's not like you, Nell. You like to get out."

"Nothing is like me anymore. We'll talk tomorrow. I know you're about to leave for the hotel."

I gave her a hug. "I love you, you know."

"I know. I'm delighted my father found you," said Nell.

"You helped make it happen," I said, giving her another squeeze. "I've always appreciated your support."

We left my bedroom together and walked outside to the pool.

"Have fun, everyone," I said. "See you later."

Vaughn came over and gave me a kiss. "Everything is fine here. Go and enjoy the wedding."

I held up the handkerchief I'd tucked into the pocket of my dress. "All set."

"You're such a romantic," Vaughn said, leaning down to kiss me again.

I noticed Bailey and Ned watching us and wondered if they saw this often at home. Or was it as bad as I thought they might be?

Back at the hotel, I met with Lauren and Annette to make sure all was ready for the wedding, reception, and dinner. After confirming that everything was in order, I walked outside to the garden where the ceremony was to take place.

Manny and his crew had done an excellent job preparing the grounds. Grass lay like a green velvet cover atop the ground. The hibiscus hedges along one side and against the hotel walls were trimmed, their pink and red blossoms creating a lovely accent.

Chairs, whose backs were covered in white linen cloth, lined up in two sections in front of the gazebo where the harpist would play behind the minister. Pale blue ribbons adorned the backs of the chairs.

As I was standing there, Danielle from *Tropical Fleurs* entered the garden, carrying an arrangement of blue hydrangeas, white roses, and white calla lilies.

"How beautiful! And so unusual," I said.

"The bride discovered blue flowers stand for not only desire and love, but also hope and the beauty around her. Very appropriate for an art teacher, don't you think?"

"Very sweet," I said. "She's become one of my favorite brides."

"Mine, too," said Danielle. "The mother of the groom not as much."

"Oh? Was there a problem?" I asked.

"She was afraid the blue wouldn't look compatible with the russet color of her dress. She wanted to make sure the blue would be soft enough." Danielle shook her head. "I talked to the bride, and we figured it out."

"This arrangement is stunning. Thank you. Rhonda and I are delighted that you're part of our wedding business group."

"Thanks. I appreciate it." Danielle finished placing the arrangement on the white altar, and then, satisfied, she left.

Studying the flowers and knowing what they signified, I thought back to Nell and Clint's wedding. It had been such a happy one. Nell was truly in love, and Clint had become overwhelmed with emotion when he saw Nell stroll into the garden on Vaughn's arm. I hoped whatever problems they were having could be resolved.

I turned as the harpist arrived with her instrument, and I helped her up the steps into the gazebo.

"Lovely day for a wedding," she said.

After a few minutes, she sat and began playing. As those pure musical notes floated above and around me, I felt my eyes water. My emotions were all over the place.

Forcing myself to concentrate on the details ahead, I hurried to my spot at the garden entrance to help guests find their seats.

I stood back as the bride appeared, looking angelic, and was then ushered into the garden by her father. Usually, Rhonda was with me. I missed her by my side as, once again, emotion overcame me.

Once the ceremony was underway, I headed into the hotel to check on the reception by the pool. We'd enlarged the pool deck to accommodate such affairs, and weather permitting, many wedding groups opted to be outdoors near the pool.

Inside the dining room, which had been partitioned, the area for the wedding dinner was ready, with baby blue linen tablecloths adorning the tables. I loved that we could offer a variety of colors for table linens to match the wedding's color theme.

Annette came over to me. "Hi, Ann. How are you doing? I spoke to Lorraine a while ago. She's devastated by Arthur's death. I think it'll be quite a while before she's ready to come back to work. I told her not to worry about it, but I'm concerned about staffing."

An idea flashed through my mind. "I think I may have someone to help out. Let's talk on Monday after the weekend is over."

"With Thanksgiving coming up, I didn't want it to be a problem," said Annette.

"You're right to bring it to my attention. What would we do without you?" I said, giving her a quick hug. Married to Bernie, she was a treasured addition to the hotel family.

Lauren joined us. "Ann, I know your daughter just arrived. Everything is set for the reception and dinner. Why don't you go home and spend time with your family? I'll see you tomorrow at the after-wedding breakfast buffet."

"Thanks. I think I'll do that. Everything seems to be running smoothly." I left and went to my car, eager to be home with Nell.

CHAPTER THREE

AT HOME, I FOUND THE KIDS PLAYING ON THE BACK LAWN with Cindy. Vaughn and Nell were sitting on the lanai.

Vaughn stood when I entered the porch. "Great! You're home early. I haven't grilled the steaks yet. You can join us for dinner."

Lauren and Annette are handling the situation at the hotel and have urged me to come home. They knew how excited I was to have Nell and the kids here."

Nell beamed at me as I took a seat on the couch next to her.

"Would you like a glass of wine before dinner?" Vaughn asked.

"I'm drinking a delicious pinot noir," said Nell. "Join me?"

"Thanks."

While Vaughn went to the kitchen to get a wine glass, I said to Nell. "I've arranged an appointment for you at the beauty salon for Monday morning. I figure we can go to lunch and shopping afterwards."

Nell's eyes filled. "Thanks. I've felt awful about myself, but was too tired to do anything about it."

"Are you feeling depressed?" I asked. "If so, we can set up an appointment with Barbara Holmes, the family psychologist."

"Perhaps later," said Nell. "I think I just needed to get away from home to a safe spot where I can really think. In fact, I've brought enough clothes for me and the kids to stay here right through the Christmas holiday."

"Clint called to tell me that. He seemed upset about it. He wanted me to help you understand that he has no choice but to work on the deal. I told him that I was willing to listen to both you and him, but that's all."

"He doesn't understand how he's changed," said Nell. "I knew he shouldn't have taken this job. It's been over two years, and my feelings haven't changed about the people he's working with. There's something so artificial about them. In a separate agreement six months ago, Clint invested money in an equity position for the special real estate deal he's working on by taking out a second mortgage. I reluctantly agreed to it because he was so excited. He's thrilled to think he might be able to do extra nice things for me and the kids if the purchase and sale of the two properties involved go through. He's even planned a surprise trip for me."

Vaughn returned to the lanai and poured wine into a glass for me, and handed Nell a plate of cheese and crackers.

"Liz called to see if you've arrived, Nell. She'll come over after dinner to see you and the kids," said Vaughn.

Nell's lips curved, highlighting her beautiful features. When we first met, I was startled by how much she looked like Liz. Seeing her like this, excited, reminded me. Somehow, we'd have to keep that smile going.

The next afternoon, Vaughn, Nell, and I got ready for Arthur's funeral service. Lorraine was hoping it would be a celebration of a life well-lived, but I wasn't the only one who thought he'd died much too soon after finding a new love with Lorraine.

The three of us arrived together at the church, where a large number of people had gathered. Lorraine was well-known in the community, and for the few years Arthur had lived here, he'd made friends too.

We sat with Liz and Chad. Soon after, Lorraine, Reggie, and Angela walked into the front of the church and sat down. Lorraine, who didn't have children of her own, sat between Angela and Reggie.

The service was short and sweet, as both Lorraine and Arthur had requested. There was no casket as Arthur had chosen to be cremated. Instead, a poster-sized photo of Arthur's smiling face was on an easel at the front of the church to remind us of the vibrant man he was.

Staring at it, I thought how fleeting life was and put my arm around Nell's shoulder in a comforting gesture. She was in a bad place. Hopefully, being in Sabal would help her straighten out her life.

Later, I joined the others as they exited the church, and we headed to Lorraine's home, where a reception had been arranged. True to her calling, Lorraine made sure the gathering was as elegant as any wedding she had planned. She offered champagne, canapés, and a variety of sandwiches and desserts, each one as appealing as the other.

The moment I found Lorraine free, I went to her and gave her a warm hug. "Again, I'm very sorry. I don't want you to feel pressured into returning to work until you're fully ready. Annette and Lauren have already spoken to me, and we have a plan to cover for you. We're all here for you."

"Thank you. This has really upended my life." She clasped her hands together as fresh tears rolled down her cheeks. "Oh, Ann, we were so happy together."

I hugged her again.

Rhonda came over to us. "Lorraine, if you need anything, please let us know. We'll be checking in on you."

Lorraine wiped her tears away. "I know, and that makes me very grateful. I'm going to take your advice and give myself lots of time off. I'll let you know when I get everything sorted out. I'm relieved you already have a plan in place."

Lorraine left, and Rhonda turned to me. "A plan in place? We do?"

"Yes," I said. "I'll tell you all about it tomorrow. Now, Vaughn is signaling to me that we need to leave. We've got to get home to Nell's children and Robbie."

Rhonda shrugged. "Okay. We'll talk tomorrow, unless I guess what it is. Then, I'll call you."

I laughed. "Deal."

At home, after changing out of our clothes into something more casual, I suggested to Nell that we take a leisurely walk through the neighborhood. Vaughn and Robbie were going to take the kids out for a short sail, and I'd have a chance to talk to Nell in private. First, I wanted to be more relaxed.

"A walk sounds delightful," said Nell.

At the mention of the word "walk", Cindy ran to the hook where her leash was kept. "Guess it's going to be a walk for all of us girls," I said, chuckling.

We said goodbye to the others and left the house. My small, gated neighborhood, with eighteen homes clustered together in a semi-private area of Sabal, was usually peaceful. Today was no exception as we strolled along the winding street. Cindy alternately lingered and then raced ahead.

"I'm grateful we have this time together," said Nell. "I've needed to talk to you. I'm very confused and upset."

I slung my arm around her shoulder. "What is it? You can tell me anything."

"On top of everything else, I think Clint might be having an affair. If so, I want a divorce," said Nell. The nostrils of her nose flared with emotion. "I hate how I look, how it makes me feel."

We stopped walking, and I faced her with a look of

concern. "That's a heavy load. Let's take it apart piece by piece and see what it looks like."

"That's probably a smart idea," she said. "It all started with Clint's new job." She stopped and shook her head. "No, it started way before then. When Clint and I first got together we were delighted to be with each other and with our lives, in general. Washington, D.C. is full of powerful people, real or imagined. We were content being ourselves, working our jobs, coming home at night. It was pretty simple. No pretense."

"I remember," I said. "Even after Bailey arrived in your lives, you were like that."

"But I wanted us to move to Florida," Nell said. "And when Ned arrived, I wanted it even more. Anyone can see how the kids seem to blossom when they're here."

"But your husband's job was in D.C.," I said.

"He promised me that at some point we'd move here," said Nell. "And then he was approached by this group of financial investors to join them. In order to do so, he had to agree to conform to their rules and appear as a successful member of the company. It wasn't enough for him to drive an SUV; he had to have a flashier car. He said it was expected of him. Then, encouraged by the people he was working with, he joined a golf club that we'd normally never be able to afford. Now, he's acting like someone I don't even know anymore."

"It doesn't sound like him," I said. "But I can see how he could get caught up in the scheme.

"One of the other investors, a rich young woman, began working with him on the special project. The one he bought equity in. Pretty soon, this project required dinners and late nights. He told me they meant nothing to him except to land the big deal."

"But?" I asked, feeling very uncomfortable and not a little frustrated with Clint.

"It feels as if he doesn't even see me or the kids anymore,

though we're standing right in front of him." Tears rolled down Nell's cheeks.

I hugged her. "It sounds like you two need some quality moments together. Why don't you suggest he stay for the entire Thanksgiving weekend? Vaughn and I will take the kids, so you can get away."

"I already suggested it. The deal is supposed to come together that weekend."

I sighed, wondering what to say. "Clint told me he doesn't want you and the kids to stay in Sabal until after the Christmas holidays. That must mean something."

"It's all for the sake of appearing to be a perfect family for PR purposes," said Nell. "I can't do that. I intend to stay here. If we do divorce, I'd want to live here anyway."

"Is a divorce what you truly want?" I asked her.

Nell shook her head. "No."

"Okay. That's a good place to start."

Nell indicated herself with a scornful sweep of her hands. "Look at me. He's working with a beautiful woman, and I've let myself go."

I felt a smile cross my face. "That, my dear, is something we can take care of. Starting tomorrow, we'll see that changes are made. Physical changes. The rest will have to come from you."

"I've felt useless and unwanted," Nell confessed, taking a deep breath to steady herself.

"I have a plan. How would you like to work at the hotel this week after your makeover, starting on Tuesday? With Lorraine off work, our hospitality department needs some help."

"Really?" Nell clapped her hands together. "That would be wonderful! That's another thing that's all wrong. Clint has wanted me to stay home with the kids, and I've missed my old job."

"Well, this will help us out and give you a new perspective. A win-win situation."

"Oh, Ann. I knew it was a lucky day when Dad met you." Nell flung her arms around me and leaned in for a cry.

My heart ached for her. She was the daughter of my heart and as beloved as my Liz.

Nell and I walked back to the house arm in arm.

"Let's celebrate a new you. How about I serve us something? Rhonda and I had Seabreeze drinks the other day, and they were light and delicious. Mostly fruit juice with just a touch of vodka."

"Sounds perfect," said Nell. "I need to relax before I plan what I want to do."

"One step at a time," I said. "Talking about sea breezes, the wind has come up, and I'm betting Vaughn and the kids will be back soon."

"Don't tell Dad everything that I've told you," Nell said. "You know how protective he can be. This is something Clint and I need to work out."

"Agreed," I said, pleased she understood that.

CHAPTER FOUR

THE NEXT MORNING, I HURRIED TO THE HOTEL FOR OUR regular Monday morning meeting. Bernie insisted he start the meeting whether Rhonda and I were there or not. And I needed to talk to Rhonda about my plan for Nell.

When I walked into the office, Rhonda was already there.

" 'Morning," I said. "I'm thankful you're here. I want to share the plan I have for the hospitality division."

She and I discussed the pros and cons of having Nell work for us and I was relieved when Rhonda agreed it was smart to have her try it out. Then she'd be ready for it if she decided to stay in Sabal and work full-time.

"Thanks," I said to Rhonda. "Nell is bored staying at home, and with both kids in school all day, she wants to do something meaningful with her freedom."

"I suppose she's like a lot of mothers who are suddenly given a day of their own. Those that don't have to work, that is," said Rhonda. "Gawd! I remember those days when Angie was headed off to college in Boston, and I was facing all those days alone."

"It was a bad time for me, and I was grateful for your offer to help me," I said. "For Nell, this is a moment in her life when she must make some life choices. I'm anxious to see what Clint has to say for himself."

"But you just said you're not going to interfere," said Rhonda.

"I've promised to be a good listener, "I said. "I owe it to both of them not to try and tell them what to do."

"Reggie is going to be taking on some of his father's

financial services clients," Rhonda said. "I hope it doesn't mean more work for Will. He was thinking of semi-retiring. Now I don't think he can. I'm trying not to say too much, but I'm worried."

"Guess we both have to take things one day at a time." I checked my watch. "We'd better run or we're going to be late."

We entered Bernie's conference room just as he was saying, "Let's get started."

When he was about to discuss the hospitality department, Bernie cleared his throat. "I have been in contact with Lorraine, and we've decided between the two of us that we won't count on her returning to her job for several weeks. We can move some employees around to accommodate her absence. If anyone has a better suggestion, let's hear it."

I raised my hand. "My daughter, Nell, is available to work this week starting tomorrow. She may be available after our Thanksgiving weekend. I'd appreciate it if you, Lauren and Annette, would be amenable to it. As you know, she's easily trainable."

"That would be marvelous," said Annette. "Is she willing to work any hours we assign her?"

"Yes," I said, understanding how important that flexibility was to that role.

"That's a temporary solution then," said Bernie. "We'll see how it goes."

"And Rhonda and I are willing to help," I said. "We're very aware of these busy times and will be available where needed."

"That brings me to another matter," said Rhonda. "We would like to remind the dining staff that, following the end of Thanksgiving dinner service, their party will begin."

"I agree," said Bernie. "It's a way to thank them and to make sure all the food is eaten. Those delicious buffet items will never be better."

As the meeting continued, I looked around the room,

realizing most of these department heads had been with us from the beginning. That made me as proud of that as some of our other achievements.

When the meeting was over, I spoke with the others in the room and then walked Rhonda back to our office.

"Okay, I'm off to be a mother to Nell. I'll make up for lost hours tomorrow," I said to Rhonda.

"No worries. Go and have a fun time," Rhonda said. "Tell Nell I said hello and welcome aboard. I'll see her tomorrow."

I left the hotel and drove home, where Nell was waiting for me. She'd already been to Hair Design for her appointment.

I entered my house, curious to see what Nell had done with her hair. Usually, she wore it shoulder-length and with a few blond highlights.

I followed Cindy into the kitchen.

Looking at Nell, I let out a sigh of admiration. "My! I love the new shorter style and the fresh blond highlights in your hair. It's perfect for your face."

Nell blushed and beamed at me. "Thank you. Melinda did such a great job. Now, I'm ready to spruce up my wardrobe. Dad gave me some money."

"That was generous of him," I said. "First, we'll have lunch and then we'll go to *Styles* and some other shops to look for new clothes for you."

"I'm already feeling better," said Nell. "Dad is taking the kids to lunch and the zoo. He was such a great father, and now he's a wonderful grandfather."

"A great man, period," I said, wrapping an arm around Nell's shoulder. "C'mon. Let's go."

Instead of sitting for a while at André's, Nell opted to go to Ken's Bar and Grill downtown for a hamburger.

"A hamburger there is a lot better than the kids' favorite place," she said, sitting in the passenger seat of my car.

"Perfect. Ken's has delicious salads, too," I said. "Tasty everything."

Sitting in a booth at Ken's, I could watch people come and go. Locals loved Ken's, and though it was busy, not many tourists were present, which made it a special gathering place.

Facing Nell, I said, "Good news. The hotel employees are delighted to have you. Rhonda says, 'Welcome Aboard'. They're ready for you to begin tomorrow. The job will entail flexible time slots, so be prepared."

Nell reached across the table and gave my hand a squeeze. "Thank you. This is going to be fabulous for me."

"I think so, too," I said. "If you decide to stay, a job at the hotel can be yours. But if you stay, what about the kids' schooling?"

"Because Bailey is in private school, I don't think it'll be an issue for her to switch to a public school. Ned is still young enough that a change shouldn't be difficult."

"Both will go to public school here?" I asked.

"Yes, it'll be much cheaper, and I know Angela's children go there," Nell said.

"Sally Kate has dyslexia and will be going to a private school, but Evan is thriving at his public school."

"That's even better, knowing there are other options," said Nell. "The important thing for Bailey and Ned is to be near family. After Clint's father died and his mother remarried, she has very little interest in our family."

"It's wise to talk about this," I said, "but we don't want to get ahead of ourselves. You and Clint need to discuss it and have some privacy together."

"I know. But for once I'm beginning to think of me and what I want," said Nell.

We finished our lunch and went to Main Street to *Styles*, the clothing shop where I bought most of my clothing.

Christine greeted us at the door and gave us each a hug. "It's nice to see you back in town," she told Nell. "And, Ann, I have some new items I think you should look at."

"Thanks. I'll look," I said, "but we're here for Nell. She needs a couple of work outfits and other items to spruce up her wardrobe."

"It's time," said Nell. "I haven't been shopping in a while and will need clothes for working at the hotel. Simple, classic dresses, skirts, and pants. Then I want a few others just for fun."

"Are you staying in town?" Christine asked Nell.

"Maybe," Nell said. "I'm working at the hotel this week. We'll see where it goes from there."

"Okay, I think I have exactly what you need. Come with me. I'm going to pull some clothes from the back."

After she showed us several items, Nell chose a number of them to try on. Nell might've complained about letting herself go, but she had the ability to make any item she wore look fantastic on her.

After a couple of hours, Nell was ready to leave with several outfits for both work and play.

Wanting to keep my focus on Nell, I asked Christine to set aside a couple of dresses for me to try on at a later time.

Bubbling with excitement, Nell left the store with me, and we headed home.

"I can't wait to show Dad what I bought," said Nell smiling at me.

"You got some bargains and a chance to shop Christine's latest arrivals. He'll be pleased for you," I said. Vaughn didn't go overboard with gifts but loved to be able to do something nice for the kids.

###

At home, Vaughn and Liana were watching Bailey and Ned swim in the pool.

Vaughn left them to greet us, and I watched his face as Nell held out what she'd bought to show him. Her excitement was matched by Vaughn's pleasure at seeing her happy.

Nell took her bags to her room, giving Vaughn and me a chance to talk privately before I went to my room to change into my bathing suit.

I was grabbing a beach towel from the linen closet when Nell approached me in tears.

"What's wrong?" I asked her.

"Clint called me and practically ordered me to fly back to D.C. with him the day after Thanksgiving. I told him no, and now he's furious with me. He told me I should've asked him about working at the hotel before agreeing to do it."

"It doesn't sound like the Clint I know and love," I said, becoming more than a little worried about the situation. "What's really going on with him? Is he under too much pressure?"

Nell shook her head. "I don't know. But now, more than ever, I'm determined to stay in Sabal."

"Understandably so," I said. "Let's try to relax and have a pleasant time. When Clint arrives on Thanksgiving, you'll have a chance to talk to him."

While Nell went to change, I joined Vaughn, Liana, and the kids at the pool.

"How is it going?" I asked Liana, who'd become like a member of our family.

"I'm doing well in school and have pretty much decided that I want to go into nursing. Vaughn has offered to help me if I don't get the scholarships I've applied for."

"Heaven knows we need more nurses," I said.

"I couldn't have even dreamed of earning my undergraduate degree without your generosity," Liana said. "I understand I'll be working here for the next week."

"Yes. We'll discuss a schedule. Nell is going to help at the hotel."

"What am I doing?" asked Nell, approaching us. "I heard you talking about me."

"I was just telling Liana that you'll be working this week," I said, as Liana and Nell gave each other a brief hug.

"Good for you, Nell," said Liana.

While the two women chatted, I slipped into the pool to play games with Bailey and Ned.

CHAPTER FIVE

THAT NIGHT, AS I LAY IN BED WITH VAUGHN, I TOLD HIM about the phone call between Nell and Clint.

"It's disturbing," Vaughn said. "And not like Clint at all. I'm hoping to take him out sailing Friday morning and have a talk with him."

"I'm trying to stay out of it, but it makes me angry to know he's treating her this way," I said. "In the meantime, working at the hotel will do her good. She's very sweet and kind, and she loves helping people. We'll need a lot of that this week."

"She seems much happier than when she first arrived. Let's keep that up," said Vaughn. He pulled me closer. "You're sweet and kind, too."

"As Nell says, it was a lucky thing for everyone in the family when we met."

As he kissed me, I thought how true that was.

The next morning, Nell and I left for the hotel together. I could sense her excitement and nerves. "No worries. You'll do fine."

"It's silly, I know, but it's been a while since I last worked, and I want to do an excellent job. To prove to myself that I can do it."

"Just be yourself," I said. "By the way, you look fabulous."

"Thanks. I feel better," Nell said.

Moments later, we entered the hotel, and after saying hello to Consuela and getting coffee, we parted ways.

I was working on the daily financial reports when Rhonda came in. "I just greeted Nell. She looks adorable. I'm delighted she's able to help us."

"I think it will do her a world of good. Especially after the phone call from Clint." I told Rhonda about it. "What do you think? You know Clint and Nell. None of this seems like them."

"They're a married couple who need a break," said Rhonda. "I know Will wants to talk to him privately. Maybe he'll find out what's really happening with Clint."

"Why does Will want to talk to Clint?" I asked.

Rhonda covered her mouth with her hand and shook her head. "I'm sorry. I wasn't supposed to mention it."

"Okay," I said. "Another piece of the puzzle."

Later, Rhonda and I made our way to the hospitality department. Even before we reached it, we heard laughter.

We entered the office and saw Lauren and Nell bent over laughing.

Delighted to see Nell like this, I couldn't help grinning, "What's funny?"

"It's the phone call Nell got," said Lauren.

"They wanted to know if we could plan a wedding for a bride who didn't have a groom," said Nell. "I was very polite about it, but said I'd have to get back to her."

"I thought it was hilarious," said Lauren. "It would be much easier to have a wedding with a groom and no bride."

"True," said Rhonda. "No Bridezilla".

We talked about some of the activities they were doing and then left to go to the housekeeping department.

We confirmed that employees were lined up for a special early morning shift the day after Thanksgiving when the hotel would magically be transformed into a holiday scene.

Rhonda and I left to talk to Laura Bakeley, a designer who'd done work for us since the beginning and had opened a Christmas decorating service we used every year. This year, the Christmas tree in the lobby was to have a silver and gold theme while the Christmas tree in the lanai and pool area would have a sea theme. The rest of the hotel would be filled with accents of greens, candles, bows, and bulbs, most following the theme.

Before I left to go home, I called Nell. "Ready to go?"

"Yes," she said. "I promised I'd come into the hotel with you tomorrow morning. I'm going to help confirm dinner reservations for Thanksgiving. We're overbooked and want to make sure everyone is still planning to come."

"Usually, there's a certain small number of people who can't make it for one reason or another. I'll meet you out back."

Nell was full of enthusiasm on our way home. "I'd forgotten how much I love to interact with people. It was an exciting day."

"Wait until Thursday night. We'll see how you feel then," I teased.

"No matter how tired I get, it'll be worth it," Nell said.

"Now, let's see how your kiddos did," I said. "Liana is amazing with children. And Papa V was pleased to spend time with them."

I called Vaughn to tell him we were on our way home.

When we drove into the driveway, Vaughn, Liana, Bailey and Ned were waiting for us with Cindy at their heels.

"Wow! What a homecoming!" I said, and then noticed a bandage on Ned's forehead.

"Oh, no!" cried Nell. As soon as the car stopped moving, she got out of it and ran to Ned.

"I missed you, Mommy," said Ned.

"Well, I'm here now," Nell said.

"What happened?" I asked Vaughn, looking on as Nell swept Ned up into her arms.

"He fell on the dock and nicked his head against a bollard. It was deep enough that the cut required four stitches. He was great at the doctor's office."

'Oh, my!" I turned to Ned. "I'm sorry you got hurt. I hear you were a very brave boy."

Ned held out his arms to me, and I took him. "Let me give you an extra hug."

He clung to me while I rocked him for a few minutes, and then he squirmed to get down.

I set him on the ground and turned to Bailey. "And what did you do today while Mommy was gone?"

Bailey's eyes lit with excitement. "Liana took me to Aunt Angie's house to play with Sally Kate. We had fun."

"I get to be with the T's tomorrow," said Ned.

"It's fun to be with family," I said.

"Come on inside," said Vaughn. "Liana has made dinner with enchiladas and burritos. We can eat anytime."

"She's such a help," I said. "She's going to make a wonderful nurse."

"I agree. She and I had a chance to talk about it. I'll fill you in later."

After changing into something comfortable, I walked out to the lanai, where Vaughn was sitting and watching the kids. On the floor, Robbie was playing a board game with Bailey and Ned. He looked up at me.

"Thanks," I said softly.

He grinned and continued playing the game.

Nell appeared and plopped down on the couch next to me. "Can we talk privately?"

"Sure. How about we take a glass of wine into my bedroom? We'll have privacy there."

"We'll be right back," I told Vaughn, though I wasn't sure how long this talk would last. Nell looked miserable.

After pouring ourselves some wine, we carried our glasses to my bedroom and onto the private patio outside. It was a favorite spot of mine.

We sat in chairs facing one another. "Here's to a successful day!" I said, lifting my glass and smiling at her.

She sighed and shrugged, then tapped her glass against mine. "Clint is going to be furious when he sees Ned. I should have been taking care of him."

I frowned. "He surely doesn't expect you to be with the children all the time, does he?"

"This is something new. All part of the family image thing," Nell said. "He wants everyone to think that instead of hiring someone to help out, I'm the perfect stay-at-home mom. I think it's because the partners in his firm all have nannies, and we can't afford one."

I set down my wine glass and stared out at the hibiscus bushes nearby, wondering what to say. The idea was preposterous. If a woman wanted that role, good for her. However, if a woman wants a career outside her home, she should be able to pursue it. It was all about having choices.

But I'd promised to be neutral and kept my mouth shut.

"You don't have to say anything, Ann. I know it's a very different attitude from what I'm used to. If I hadn't had a good-paying job, we could never have afforded our first house, even with the financial help you and Dad gave us."

"Why is Clint acting this way?" I asked her, puzzled by all the changes.

Nell emitted a long sigh and looked down at the floor. When she lifted her face, there were tears in her eyes. He's invested all our money in this equity position opportunity.

He's afraid of stepping out of line. If he can make it work, we'll be very successful. Financially."

"What a mistake," I muttered before I could stop myself.

"It really is," Nell said. "I realize how important it is for me to make him see that all this pressure he's putting on himself is ruining our lives together."

"Can you persuade him to stay longer than Friday night?" I asked.

"We'll see." Nell gave me a weak smile. "I'm grateful you and Dad are willing to have the kids and me here."

"Of course. We love you," I said, reaching out and clasping her hand. "We're here for you."

"I'm not going back to D.C. until Clint and I have a clear understanding about our future together," said Nell.

"You can stay here for as long as you need to," I said.

"Thanks," said Nell, standing. "Now, I need to be with my children."

Later, at dinner, I was pleased to see how cheerful the kids were as we ate Liana's delicious food. The kids' chatter was very interesting. Though they spoke of friends and happenings at home, Clint's name was never mentioned. I found that telling.

After dinner, Bailey and Ned were put to bed, and Vaughn, Nell, and I sat on the lanai. As if the dog knew she needed extra support, Cindy curled herself into Nell's lap.

After discussing Clint's situation, Vaughn offered to call and invite him for a weekend of sailing.

"You can try," said Nell. "But I'd be surprised if he agrees to do it. Not when he's working with Claudine on their special project. Claudine Everett's family made a fortune in oil and real estate, and she's not only rich but beautiful," Nell explained.

"What is this project?" Vaughn asked.

"It has to do with an investment in a startup company that will be sold. Something like that," Nell said.

"I wonder if Will or Reggie has heard any news about it," I said. "Or maybe one of Arthur's clients that Reggie will be handling from now on."

"Let's keep it as simple as possible," Vaughn said. "To me, it sounds like a deal that could go terribly wrong."

Nell's cell phone rang. She looked at it and stood. "It's Clint. I'll go talk to him in private."

After she left the room, Vaughn looked at me and shook his head. "I don't like what I'm hearing."

"Me, either," I said. "But we have to let them figure it out for themselves."

"Okay, but I still don't like it," he said.

A few minutes later, Nell came back into the room. "I asked Clint if he could extend his stay to include the entire weekend, but he said no. He's hoping for a sail with you on Friday, Dad, before his evening flight."

"Weather permitting, we'll go," Vaughn said. "Maybe I can get a better understanding of what's going on."

CHAPTER SIX

THE NEXT MORNING, NELL AND I LEFT FOR THE HOTEL, promising to have lunch with the kids in my office. Bailey and Ned loved visiting the hotel, and I always made sure they had a treat while they were there.

The Wednesday before Thanksgiving was busy throughout the hotel with guests arriving from out of town for the weekend to celebrate not only Thanksgiving but the conversion of the hotel to activities for the Christmas holidays. We were scheduled to have our first high tea that Friday afternoon.

After seeing Nell off to her part of the hotel, I stopped in the kitchen to speak with Consuela. She was the mother I'd never had, and I could talk to her about anything.

" 'Morning," she said, automatically handing me a cup of coffee. "How are you?"

"I need some advice. Nell is working at the hotel for a few days, maybe longer. I'm worried about her, about her relationship with Clint. But I don't want to say too much. Isn't that what you'd advise?"

"It's a thin line," said Consuela. "As long as nobody is getting physically hurt, it's best to let them work it out. Too often, parents may choose to speak up and then find themselves being left out after the situation changes."

I hugged her. "Thanks. That's what I thought. You're very understanding to your family. They adore you, as we all do at the hotel."

"Just be kind," said Consuela. "Like you usually are. Are

you ready for the rush tomorrow and the beginning of the Christmas holidays?"

"As ready as we'll ever be. I understand we're overbooked for dinners all day, but I'm sure it will be straightened out by the end of today."

"More and more people are flying in for the weekend. It's helpful that Sabal has festivities downtown at this time," said Consuela.

"That certainly helps us," I said. "Thanks for the coffee. See you later. Nell's children, Bailey and Ned, are coming to my office for lunch. I'm sure they won't want to miss you."

Smiling, she gave me a little wave. "See you all later."

When I walked into the office, Rhonda was there at her desk. "We're going to have to juggle guest rooms. The reservations office sent us a list of changes to look over."

While we wanted everyone to be satisfied, we remained loyal to our guests who returned year after year and tried not to disrupt their requests.

We were busy later, reviewing promo information for the holidays, when Vaughn arrived with Bailey and Ned.

"We're here for lunch," said Bailey, twirling around in the new sundress I'd bought her.

Ned followed behind her and came right over to Rhonda and me.

"What happened to your head?" asked Rhonda, swooping him up into her lap. The bandage had been changed to a regular Band-Aid.

"I bumped my head," said Ned. "But I was very brave."

"Of course you were," said Rhonda, hugging him. She set him down to take Bailey into her arms. "Such a pretty dress. Are you having fun with Grandpa?"

Bailey glanced at Vaughn. "Grandpa lets us swim in the pool for as long as we want and gives us treats."

I looked at Vaughn's sheepish expression and laughed.

Kids didn't let you get away with anything.

"Come sit at the conference table, and I'll call Nell to tell her you're here." After reaching Nell, I left the office to get our lunch. The rule for hotel lunches was to taste everything.

When I returned to the office with sandwiches, salads, cake, and fruit, I took a moment to focus on my family, who were waiting patiently at the conference table. Pleased, I tucked away the image as a sweet memory.

Nell sat holding Ned on her lap. Vaughn and Bailey were looking at a picture she'd drawn on a blank piece of computer paper. Rhonda was standing by, talking to Nell.

"Here's lunch. Auntie Rhonda, will you join us? I said.

"Of course. I'm sure it's yummy. Right, kids?"

Bailey and Ned nodded and leaned forward as I opened the two boxes I'd picked up in the kitchen. "Consuela said to say hi. Before you leave, you can stop in the kitchen to say hello to her."

"I'll get the drinks," said Rhonda. "Lemonade for everyone?"

"Yes," said Nell. "That would be great."

Vaughn and I quickly agreed.

I placed the sandwiches and salads in the middle of the table and handed out paper plates and napkins.

"I like picnics at the hotel," announced Bailey.

"It's fun to have you here," I said. "And tomorrow you get to come to the hotel for turkey."

"Can I have a big piece of turkey? I like turkey," said Ned, giving a dubious look at one of the green salads.

"Of course," I said and exchanged amused smiles with Vaughn.

Rhonda returned with Consuela and the drinks. After Consuela exchanged hugs with the kids, we sat down to eat our lunch. The kitchen had packed peanut butter and jelly sandwiches along with other items, and everyone was pleased with their choices.

"Is Daddy coming to Florida?" asked Bailey.

"He'll be here tomorrow," Nell said, giving Bailey an overly bright smile. "He's busy at work."

"He's always busy at work," Bailey said. "I like being with Grandpa."

"Who's getting ready for dessert?" I asked, veering attention away from Clint's absence.

Nell shot me a look of gratitude, but we all were uneasy about Bailey's awareness.

After lunch, we trooped into the kitchen to say hello to Jean-Luc, and then Nell took the kids on a tour of the hotel and to her office in the hospitality department.

Vaughn and I walked out to the pool and lanai area for a private moment.

"I was able to get in touch with Clint to ask him if he could extend his stay," he told me. "He said he was flying to Sabal in the company's private jet and would arrive around noon tomorrow. He thought he could arrange to leave Saturday morning instead of Friday night."

"Private jet? He's certainly living a glamorous lifestyle," I said. "I'm worried about it."

"Me, too," said Vaughn.

Nell returned with the kids and said, "I have to take over for Lauren so she can go to lunch. See you all later." She kissed each child and left.

Watching the spring in her step, I couldn't help but think of all the positive changes she had undergone in the last few days, and I wondered what Clint would think of them.

The next morning, as Nell and I got ready to leave for the hotel, I said goodbye to Vaughn and the little kids. Robbie was still asleep. "Liana will be here shortly. Have a fun day. We'll see you at the hotel for your 'turkey day'."

"I like turkey," said Ned, and I chuckled. At our hotel lunch, he'd been a sport about tasting a salad he definitely didn't like.

Nell appeared, looking adorable in a dark-green linen dress that added a touch of green to her blue eyes.

"Remember to wear comfortable shoes," I said. "You'll be doing a lot of standing to greet guests and will be helping them get seated for dinner." In addition to breakfast for hotel guests, we had three seatings for our Thanksgiving buffet. It made a very long day.

Nell took off the pretty high heels she'd chosen and went back to her room to get the practical black heels I'd insisted on buying for her.

"Don't worry about picking up Clint at the airport," said Vaughn. "I've already arranged to do that."

"Thanks, Dad." Nell gave him a hug. "Tell him I'll see him when he comes to the hotel."

"Okay, will do," said Vaughn, giving me a look of surprise.

I kissed him before stealing another hug from Bailey and Ned.

In the car on the way to the hotel, I turned to Nell. "You can leave the hotel to greet Clint if you'd like to."

Nell shook her head. "No, I don't want to have any disagreements. It'll be safer for both of us to meet at the hotel. Any arguments can be handled at home. I'm sure he's going to be upset that Ned got hurt."

"That doesn't sound like Clint. Kids get hurt occasionally. It's nothing serious."

Ned gave me a worried look, and I let it go.

Rhonda and I were greeting guests in the lobby when my

cell phone chimed. *Vaughn.* I picked up the call.

"Liana and I are busy cleaning up the kids after a finger painting session that Liana conducted with them. Clint called to say they were landing at the airport. Can you leave and pick him up?"

"Sure. I'm curious to see this private jet he's flying in," I said, knowing that wasn't the only thing I was curious about.

Quietly, I told Rhonda what I was doing and left the hotel to go to the Sabal airport. As I drove the short distance, I couldn't help but remember the first time I saw it when Liz and I flew to Sabal to spend Thanksgiving with Rhonda and Angela. A lot has happened since then. Most of them were good, some not wonderful.

I pulled into the parking lot as a sleek jet came down the runway. I hurried into the terminal and stood at the gate waiting for Clint to disembark. There was no crowd waiting for others with me. I got a clear look at a dark-haired woman descending the airstair before Clint appeared wearing a golf shirt and tan slacks. He was a tall, handsome man with butterscotch hair and sparkling hazel eyes behind his sunglasses.

They walked toward me, smiling and talking to one another in a way that disturbed me. My mothering instinct rose inside me, filling me with anxiety. They looked like a couple.

They entered the building. "Hi, Ann. Where's Vaughn? Claudine is looking forward to meeting him."

"Hi, Clint. Vaughn couldn't make it. That's why I'm here." I turned my gaze to the woman beside him. Tall, thin, and with thick, glossy, black hair that fell in a straight line to her shoulders, she stared at me with brown eyes that were busy sizing me up.

"Ann Sanders, this is Claudine Everett, one of my business associates," said Clint. "She and I have been heading up a big project for our company."

"Hello," I said, holding out my hand.

Claudine gripped my hand almost painfully. "Nice to meet you. I'm disappointed. When I pick up Clint Saturday morning, I hope Vaughn will be here." It was a command.

Startled by such boldness, 1 blinked and stepped back. "That depends on my husband's schedule."

Claudine's lips tightened. "Well, I'd better go. My family is waiting for me at our winter home in Miami." Claudine turned and gave Clint a hug. "See you Saturday."

"Okay," said Clint. "Saturday at ten. But I still think we can work in Florida this weekend."

Claudine shook her head. "No, the rest of the team is in D.C. They expect us there. And we need to work together without any interruptions. Goodbye, Mrs. Sanders." She turned and walked away from us with a confident posture and sure steps.

Clint noticed the confusion on my face and said, "I'm sorry this project has ruined my usual Thanksgiving stay. As I keep trying to explain to Nell, it could mean a very big profit for the company and me, in particular."

"Does it really matter that much?" I asked.

Clints cheeks flushed. "This is a chance to prove myself capable in a way I haven't been able to before. It's for Nell and the kids."

"But mostly for you," I said, unable to hold back.

Clint frowned and looked away before turning back to me. "Why is Nell working for you? I make enough money that she doesn't have to do that," he said with an edge to his voice.

"I'll let you discuss that with her," I said. "But I will say that we're grateful for her help. As you may know, Arthur Smythe died recently and his wife, Lorraine, who heads our wedding service, will be out for some time."

"Ah, yes. I was sorry to hear about that. I talked to Arthur a while ago after I got my new job. He was a great guy," said Clint.

"We're all sad about it," I said. "Though he'd been ill, it was still unexpected."

"I'll call Reggie while I'm here," said Clint, sounding more like the son-in-law I loved.

I drove Clint to the house, and Vaughn and I stood by as Clint greeted the kids.

Seeing him greet Bailey and Ned with heartfelt hugs and kisses, I felt a sense of relief about him.

"Whoa! Ned, how'd you get hurt, Bud? Where was Mommy?" Clint asked him.

"Mommy works at the hotel," Bailey said proudly.

"Well, I'm back now, and she doesn't need to do that," Clint said.

"We like the hotel," said Ned.

"Yes, it's a beautiful place," said Clint, turning to us. "After I get settled, I'll drive to the hotel to see Nell."

"I'm off to work," I said. "See you later."

Vaughn walked me out to my car.

"I met Clint's business partner, Claudine Everett. She wants you to drop Clint off at the airport on Saturday so she can meet you. She's definitely a woman who knows what she wants. And I think it might be Clint."

"You don't like her," said Vaughn.

"Seeing the way she and Clint were acting and her dismissive manner toward me, I'm not a fan. No wonder she makes Nell feel insecure. I love Nell, and I'm afraid she's going to be hurt more than she has been."

Vaughn's lips thinned. "I'm going to try and find out why Clint is acting this way."

"Nell has told me some things, but you might have a better chance of getting information from Clint than I can. As we've promised one another, we can get information, but we have to let them work it out."

"Right," said Vaughn. "But nobody is going to carelessly hurt my daughter."

I headed to the hotel to a different Thanksgiving than I'd thought we'd have.

CHAPTER SEVEN

When I walked into the lobby, I saw Nell greeting guests arriving for the first dinner session. Seeing her chatting with them, I was reminded of the stressed woman who'd arrived a few days earlier. After speaking with Clint, I hoped they would find a healthy solution to their problems, but I wasn't pleased with his new attitude. Nell noticed me and came over. "How's Clint? Has he seen the children?"

"Clint is fine. He's seen the children and is getting settled now," I said. "He's coming by the hotel to say hello to you."

"Oh, good. I want him to see how much I enjoy helping out here," said Nell.

I gave her a quick hug and went to the kitchen to see what was happening there. Thanksgiving might be a holiday for other people, but for the staff at the hotel, it was one of the busiest days of the year, if not *the* busiest.

Being careful to stay out of the way, I watched as the kitchen crew worked together like various sections of a symphony orchestra. As many parts of the meal as possible had been prepared ahead of time.

Annette stood by helping the servers maintain a steady stream of comings and goings from the kitchen, keeping a well-stocked supply of food on display at the buffet stations bordering the dining room walls.

"How's it going?" I asked her.

"Smoothly," she replied. "I'm always amazed by how much people eat at these dinners."

Waving goodbye, I thought of Robbie. He saved up room

in his stomach all day so he could enjoy eating as much as he could at the Thanksgiving feast.

I left her to take my turn greeting guests at the dining room door. From there, I would oversee staff seating guests and taking orders for drinks. The attention to detail was worthwhile. We'd had our Thanksgiving meals featured in several local society and tourist magazines and online forums, which boosted dining room sales throughout our high season.

Nell approached me. "I saw Clint, and we've agreed to talk alone during this visit. He told me he's going sailing with Dad tomorrow. I think that'll be nice for both of them."

"Oh, I'm glad," I said, determined not to mention my concern about the way Clint acted around Claudine.

When Vaughn, Clint, Liana, and all three kids showed up for dinner, I was beginning to feel exhausted by the effort of being on my feet greeting people. But when I saw them, I gave each of them a genuine smile.

Nell took her break to join the family, and I kept an eye on them from a distance as they ate together. Liana had done a nice job of seeing that Bailey and Ned were wearing their holiday "outfits". They looked adorable.

Some diners approached Vaughn for autographs, but most were kind enough to stay away. Studying him, I remembered how intimidated I'd been by him when we first met. But then, as he was now, he was very kind to all who approached him.

"Looks like another success," said Rhonda, coming up to me. "One more seating and we'll be done. I don't know about you, Annie, but my feet are killing me."

"Go have a rest in our private spot," I said. "We have time between the seatings for you to have a break. I'll join you when I can."

"Clint looks good. Tired, but fine," said Rhonda. "And our Nell is adorable in that cute dress as she speaks to diners."

I loved that Rhonda and I considered all the kids as ours together.

Clint rose from his chair and headed to me, holding his phone. "Ann, is there a place where I can talk privately?"

"You can use my office," I said. "Follow me."

"Okay, I'm on my way to a private location," Clint said into his phone as he walked behind me. "Claudine, I can't change my plans."

I showed him into my office and left him there, wondering why Claudine would be calling him on this family holiday.

When I caught up to him later, I said, "Is everything alright?"

He sighed. "Yes. I'm still staying here until Saturday morning."

I gave him a look of approval. "Great. We've all missed your regular week with us."

"I know," he said. "It's been really busy with the project."

I gazed up at him, but he looked away.

Letting out a sigh of worry, I said nothing.

After the last group of guests had finished their meals, things happened quickly. The dining room was closed, and servers and other staff descended upon the food on the buffet table even as more food was brought in. We allowed them to drink beer or wine on the premises three times during the year. This was one of those times, along with our Christmas employee party and the New Year's Eve event for those who had worked at the party. Now, this was a great way to thank those who had devoted themselves all day to making our Thanksgiving a success. Jean-Luc, Bernie, Annette, Consuela, and other department heads joined in, making it a boost for morale.

Rhonda and I circulated, thanking them for their help, too tired to think of staying and eating more than a snack. After sampling the food all day, I'd had enough. I noticed that Nell had already left.

At home, Bailey and Ned were already in bed, and Robbie was playing games in his room. Vaughn was sitting alone on the lanai.

"Hi. Where are Nell and Clint?" I asked him.

"They've gone for a walk. They had a disagreement about the kids' bedtime, and they wanted to have some privacy."

I sat beside him on the couch and wiggled my toes out of my shoes. "Ah, that feels delightful."

"It looked like another success at The Beach House Hotel," said Vaughn, drawing me into his arms.

I leaned gratefully against him. "Thanks. It was. The employees were celebrating when I left. They did a great job. How were Nell and Clint at dinner? I know she couldn't stay at the table for very long, but were they all right?"

"I think so," said Vaughn. "Then Clint got that phone call. But it seemed fine when he told Nell he was still staying until Saturday morning."

"That phone call was from Claudine. I don't trust her. Clint is an attractive man, and she seems to like having him at her beck and call. It seems strange that she insists on having him work with her over a holiday weekend."

"I agree," said Vaughn. "We'll have to see what happens next. Clint has promised to head out on the water with me mid-morning. Before then, he's going to meet Reggie for coffee to offer his condolences."

"Yes, he told me he wants to do that," I said, looking up when Nell and Clint walked into the room.

"Hi, Ann. Dinner was delicious. Another success for you,"

said Clint.

"And for the staff," I said. "But thank you. I'm elated you could make it."

"He tells me he can't stay the weekend," Nell said tersely. "But at least he's here now."

Clint studied Nell and then sighed. "I'll make it up to you at Christmas."

"I've told Clint that I'm going to remain here in Sabal until after the Christmas holidays. I've talked to him about doing it for a while, and I've decided it will give him space to work on that special project of his."

Looking uncertain, Clint shrugged. "The kids love it here. I get it."

"We'd all better get to bed early," I told them. "It's a busy day tomorrow. Nell, you and I will leave by seven at the latest."

"What's going on?" Clint asked me.

"The hotel is transformed into Christmas first thing in the morning. Selected employees help our designer put up decorations, lights, and trees, so when guests come down to the dining room for breakfast, it seems like magic."

"You remember how the kids and I would always come to the hotel to see the change," said Nell. "To them, it's always been magical."

Clint put an arm around Nell. "See you tomorrow."

Nell blew Vaughn and me little kisses and went with Clint to the guest wing of the house.

Vaughn and I looked at one another. It was obvious the walk had helped Nell and Clint.

"I'm ready for bed, too," said Vaughn, getting to his feet.

"Sounds fine to me." I went to Robbie's room. Cindy was curled up on the bed with him as he lay against the pillow with his earphones on.

I caught his attention and kissed him on the cheek.

After turning out all the lights in the rest of the house, I went to my bedroom, too tired to do much but strip down and crawl into bed.

The next morning, the thought of the hotel's Christmas surprise for our guests got me out of bed. I moved quickly and quietly to get ready for the day.

When I went into the kitchen, Nell was already there, dressed in a beautiful red silk blouse and black slacks.

"Dressed for the holiday, I see. That looks great on you," I said.

She smiled and took another sip of coffee. "Thanks. I wanted to fit in."

I put my arm around her. "You fit in perfectly anytime. Have a good sleep?"

"Surprisingly, yes," she said.

"Today, we're going to host our first high tea of the season, and I thought you'd be perfect to oversee it, along with Lauren or Annette."

"Lauren and I are already planning on doing it," said Nell. "I really like her."

"She's a very pleasant, hardworking person. We're lucky to have her."

We left for the hotel without disturbing anyone else.

On the way to the hotel, I asked Nell if she and Clint were able to talk to each other.

She shrugged. "I guess. He says he loves me and is doing this for our future, but there's something he's not telling me. I'm sure of it."

"Maybe after this big deal of his is concluded, you can get away. Just the two of you," I said.

"Yes, we've agreed to do that. And though he doesn't like it, he knows the kids and I are staying in Florida. I told him that was non-negotiable."

"You know you're welcome to stay with your dad and me for as long as you want," I said.

"I appreciate that because it gives me the flexibility I need. I love working at the hotel."

"Rhonda and I are pleased about that," I said, and pulled through the gates to the hotel. I stopped and stared at the twinkling white lights shining from the landscaping at the base of the hotel and around the trunks of the palm trees.

"It's gorgeous," gushed Nell, in awe.

"Manny and his crew must have started before daylight to put the lights up," I said.

When I pulled around to the back parking lot, I noticed Manny and his men still working on outdoor lighting.

Rhonda's car and Laura Bakeley's van were already parked in the lot.

Nell and I got out of the car, walked through the back of the hotel, and hurried to the lobby to see the work there.

A huge spruce tree stood in the middle of the space. It had already been strung with white lights, and three people were hanging silver and gold balls and ornaments on the tree. Other crew members were placing greens with gold and silver ribbons in various locations throughout the lobby, along with candles or flowers. I knew this was just the beginning. By the end of the day, every area would be "dressed" for the holidays.

I left Nell there and went outside to the lanai and pool area. A smaller tree had been set up with white lights, and two people were hanging ornaments that were part of Laura's seaside theme. Mermaids, birds, seashells, and starfish were all part of the decorations.

When I went to check the dining room, I saw boxes of decorations waiting. Under Annette's supervision, a highly coordinated effort was made between Laura's team, our housekeeping department, and the dining staff.

I stopped in the kitchen for my usual cup of coffee and happily accepted a Christmas cookie from Consuela. "How are you?" I asked. "Recovered from yesterday?"

She laughed. "Not for another day or two."

After a quick hug, I went into the office where Rhonda was sitting, staring at the computer. "Angie and Liz have updated the website for the holidays, and it looks smashing."

"Do we know yet how many people were served dinner yesterday?" I asked her.

"Almost four hundred people," she said.

"That's amazing," I said. "The lobby is going to be stunning. Even though it's a lot of work to make the process run smoothly, I love the holidays."

"My Christmases growing up were about holiday food. Not the presents," said Rhonda. "We didn't have much, but we celebrated what we had."

"I bet they were fun. Mine were pretty unexciting except for friends' parties," I said. "I guess that's why I love being here at the hotel with everyone. Let's go see where Laura wants us to help."

When we found Laura, she was on top of a ladder in the lobby. She saw us and climbed down. "Will you two handle decorating the tree on the lanai? Two people are there now, but they need help, and I want it done to your satisfaction."

"Sure thing," Rhonda said, and I followed her outside to the sheltered spot to see what needed to be done. Guests typically arrived at the pool early to reserve poolside chairs. We hoped the decorating would be cleaned up before then.

Outside, working with the others, I lifted one ornament after another, placing it strategically on the tree. I inhaled the smell of pine and lifted my face to the sun. Some people couldn't imagine celebrating the holiday in a warm place, but I loved it. Though most of the snowmen were inflated, it was fun to see how different families celebrated. Nothing was more beautiful to me than seeing the trunks of palm trees wrapped in white lights.

Early morning, Vaughn phoned to say goodbye. "I'm planning on heading north toward Tampa on the boat," he said. "I've got enough food and drinks for both lunch and supper, if we choose to stay out late. It should be a great sail. The sea breezes are in our favor."

"Have a great time," I said. "I hope you get the chance to talk to Clint and find out what's really going on with him."

"That's my goal," said Vaughn. "Here he is now. I love you, Ann. See you later."

"Love you, too," I said. "Have fun, but be safe!"

I ended my call with Vaughn and looked up as Nell joined me. "Vaughn and Clint should have a great sailing day," she said. "Clint's excited. He called to tell me they're getting ready to leave."

"That's sweet," I said. "I had the chance to wish Vaughn a safe trip."

Nell clasped her hands. "I'm hoping being here with you and Dad will help Clint see how he's changed. Dad tells it like it is. Maybe talking to him will help Clint."

"I hope so, too."

Once the Christmas decorations were up, Rhonda and I met with Nell and Lauren to set up the library for our first high tea.

"It's a special event for all ages but especially for women with friends or family," I said. "Rhonda and I ordered special dinnerware for the event, and it adds to the ambiance." I held up a thin teacup decorated with flowers that matched the pink tablecloths on the tables for two, four, or six people.

"One of the women on the dining staff or a member of the

local theater dresses up in costume for the occasion," Lauren told Nell.

Printed menus had already been placed on each table describing the choices of tea or coffee and listing the sandwiches and sweets.

"I love it," said Nell. "I can't wait to bring Bailey here this year."

"It's a favorite for mothers and daughters to do, regardless of their ages," I said.

"I'm excited that I'm staying here to participate," said Nell. She checked her watch. "I'd better call Liana to check on the kids."

"You've seen the layout. Why don't you go home to be with them? Lauren and I can handle the tea."

"Right," said Lauren. "Thanks for your help, Nell."

Making sure guests were enjoying the tea was something that I enjoyed doing. And it would take my mind off my worries.

Later, after seeing that the tea was going well, I went to my office to check in with Rhonda.

"I'm ready to go home," she said. "Next week is going to be busy with not one wedding but two."

"As soon as the tea service wraps up, I'll leave," I said. "Have a nice evening."

"You, too," she said. "See you tomorrow."

At home, I found Nell in the pool with Bailey and Ned. Cindy was standing nearby, watching them. Robbie was stretched out in a lounge chair.

"Hi," said Nell. "The water's great. Come on in."

"I'll be right there. I'm ready for some downtime." I went inside to change my clothes, eager to relax.

I'd just put on my swimsuit when my cell rang. *Vaughn.*

Frowning, I picked up the call. "Hi, Vaughn. What's up?"

"There's been a terrible accident," he said. "Clint and I have been taken to the Tampa General Hospital. You and Nell better come up."

CHAPTER EIGHT

Holding onto my cell phone, I felt my knees get weak and lowered myself onto the bed. "Who's hurt? What happened?"

"I'm fine, but Clint has been injured," said Vaughn.

"What? How in the world did that happen?" I asked.

"A speedboat of drug smugglers being chased by the Coast Guard almost hit us. I'll tell you the details as you drive up here," said Vaughn in a shaky voice. "I'm still trying to process it. Be sure to tell Nell that, aside from being injured, Clint will be okay.

"I'll phone you when we're on our way," I said, my mind racing as I ended the call. I knew we'd have to be calm. Maybe Stephanie and Randolph Willis could come over to help Robbie with the kids. She and her husband, Randolph, had been adopted as grandparents one Christmas when they couldn't get a room at the hotel and spent the holiday with Vaughn, Robbie, and me. They'd do anything for us.

Sure enough, as soon as I asked Stephanie if she could stay with the kids, she agreed and promised to come over right away. That worry taken care of, I went to the lanai and asked Nell to please come inside.

She looked surprised but got out of the pool, wrapped a towel around herself, and walked over to me.

Studying me, she said, "What's wrong? You look upset."

"Come into the kitchen with me and have a seat," I said, not wanting to frighten the children.

"What is it? Is it Clint? Dad?" she asked as she hurried

into the kitchen and stood by the table.

"I just got a call from Vaughn. Clint is all right except there's been an accident and he's injured. They're at Tampa General Hospital. We need to drive up there now. As we travel, Vaughn will give us more details. All I know is that it involved a smuggler's speedboat and the Coast Guard."

"Oh my God!" Nell clapped her hand over her mouth and looked up at me with tears flooding her eyes.

I put my hand on her shoulder. "I've called Stephanie, and she and Randolph are coming over to stay with the kids. Please get dressed, and we'll drive to Tampa right away. Better pack an overnight bag in case we have to stay."

I went into my bedroom to change clothes.

As I was leaving the room, Stephanie and Randolph arrived. Nell was outside explaining to Bailey, Ned, and Robbie what was going to happen.

Stephanie and Randolph followed me outside.

Robbie's face lit up at the sight of them. "Hi. Bailey and Ned, do you remember my honorary grandparents—Grandma Steph and Grandpa Randolph?"

"Yes," said Bailey. "We baked Christmas cookies together one time."

"That's right," said Stephanie. She turned to Ned. "And if I remember correctly, you ate a lot of icing."

Ned grinned.

"Okay," said Nell, coming to stand beside me, trying to remain calm. "We're leaving now, kids. Have fun with Robbie and our special grandparents. We'll see you later."

Carrying overnight bags, Nell and I walked away before any of us could become too emotional.

"I'll drive," I said, eliminating any need to discuss it.

I grabbed bottles of water to take with us and led the way to my SUV. The automobile had the latest features, and I'd be able to talk through the car's audio system and drive at the same time. I was eager to hear more details of Vaughn's dreadful news.

Once Nell and I were in the car, and we'd left the house, Nell let her tears come. "What if Clint is severely injured and won't have a normal life? Or worse yet, dies. I couldn't bear it if I lost him. I really love him, you know."

"Let's not panic, sweetheart. If Vaughn says Clint is going to be okay, I believe him. But, like you, I want to see him with my own eyes and know exactly what's wrong with him."

I called Vaughn to tell him we were on our way. Through the car's speaker, I asked him for more details.

"We were headed toward Tampa, as I told you we would," said Vaughn. "The breeze was good, and we were moving along smoothly under sail, making excellent time. We decided to put up the spinnaker. I was at the wheel while Clint was on the foredeck, holding onto the spinnaker. Seemingly out of nowhere, a speedboat heads right toward us, coming like a bat out of hell. He didn't notice us and our position until the last minute. I turned the wheel to avoid a crash, and Clint fell against the life rail and overboard."

"What happened to him?"

"He was holding onto the spinnaker, and his arms hit the life rail before he went over. I was trying to get back to him, throw him a lifesaver, when another speedboat driven by the Coast Guard went to Clint's aid. I don't know what would've happened to him if they hadn't been right there. Both his arms are broken, and he was having trouble staying afloat."

Nell clapped a hand to her mouth. Tears rolled down her cheeks.

"So, this was part of a smuggling scene?" I asked.

"Yes. It apparently happens more than one would think along the Florida coastlines," Vaughn said. "We were just lucky the boat didn't hit us."

"How bad are Clint's arms?" asked Nell.

"His right forearm has been broken in one place. His left arm is broken in two places. They're operating now to set it," said Vaughn. "The orthopedic surgeon can give you the medical details when you arrive."

"It sounds awful," I said.

"How is he going to be able to handle two broken arms?" Nell said. "One is bad enough."

You'll be able to discuss everything with the doctor, Nell. I'm very grateful for the rescue and the excellent medical care. But as you can imagine, I feel terrible about the accident."

"Where's the boat?" I asked.

"It's at a dock near the Tampa Convention Center. It was towed there while l accompanied Clint to the hospital. Thank God for all the help we received."

"I'll say. You weren't hurt?"

"Just some bruising on my legs," said Vaughn. "When you arrive at the hospital, ask for the Orthopedic Trauma Center. It's a 24-bed unit. I'm in the waiting area. I'll meet you there."

"We're driving as fast as we can," I said. "Be sure to keep yourself hydrated and get some food if you need it."

"Okay," said Vaughn. "Don't worry, Nell. I'm staying right near Clint. The surgery may be over by the time you get here. He might even be awake to see you. We've been here for a while. I didn't want to let you know until I knew what exactly to tell you."

Vaughn ended the call, and Nell and I simultaneously let out puffs of worry.

"How's Clint going to be able to handle his recovery?" asked Nell. "He won't be able to use the computer or write for a while. And performing basic tasks is going to be difficult. He'll have to stay in Sabal with us, where he can get the best help."

She and I exchanged glances.

"Maybe some good will come out of this," I said. "He

won't be able to fly back to D.C. tomorrow like Claudine wants."

"No, even he will see that isn't wise," said Nell. "He and I had a chance to begin talking about our problems. Maybe Clint being forced to stay in Sabal will prove to be helpful to both of us."

"What if he wants you to go back to D.C. to help him?" I asked.

"We'll have to work something out because I'm staying in Sabal no matter what. It's important for the kids and for me to have a choice."

I didn't say anything, but inwardly, I agreed Nell should have some say in her future. I just hoped they'd see the value of what they had together. But only time would tell.

CHAPTER NINE

When Nell and I walked into the surgical waiting room and saw Vaughn, both of us rushed forward into his embrace.

"How's Clint?" Nell asked, giving him a teary look.

"A nurse told me he's in the recovery room and a doctor will come to speak to us shortly," said Vaughn. "I explained you were on your way."

A man wearing green scrubs approached us. "Are you Clint Dawson's family?"

At our response, he shook hands with each of us. "I'm Dr. Taunton."

"I'm his wife, Nell," she said. "How is he?"

"He fractured both arms. His right arm suffered a clean break in the ulna and is being taken care of with a lower-arm cast, sling, ice, and rest. The left arm, however, required reduction surgery to realign the broken humerus in the upper arm. We also performed internal fixation on that bone, which involves placing metal pieces within the bone to hold it in place while it heals. The left arm also had a less severe fracture of the radius in the lower arm. Clint told me he's right-handed, which makes it helpful."

"What are we talking about in healing time?" I asked.

"It takes approximately twelve weeks for a broken arm to heal," said Dr. Taunton. "However, it can take up to two years to regain full use, strength, and motion in a fractured arm that requires surgery. It's normal to have some pain for two to three weeks and mild pain for up to six weeks after surgery."

"Does he have to wear a cast on his left arm?" asked Vaughn.

"He'll have to wear a full cast for at least a few weeks," said Dr. Taunton. "And he may feel tired and run down because his body will be working hard to heal itself. Fortunately, Clint is healthy and has a strong body."

"When can he come home?" Nell asked.

"I'd like to see him stay here overnight to allow us to monitor how he's doing," Dr. Taunton said. "A rehabilitation nurse will speak to him in the morning about what he should and shouldn't do in the weeks ahead."

"Can I see him?" asked Nell.

Dr. Taunton checked his watch. "I believe he's in the unit by now. Sure, go ahead."

"Thank you, Doctor," said Nell before rushing away.

Dr. Taunton, Vaughn, and I smiled at her hasty departure.

"Thank you, Dr. Taunton," I said. "It's a relief to know he's in capable hands."

"The first aid given to him by the Coast Guard team was helpful," Dr. Taunton said. He turned to Vaughn. "I'm sorry this happened to you."

Vaughn let out a worried sigh. "Me, too. It was an accident that should never have occurred."

"Is it okay for more than one family member to see Clint?" I asked.

"Of course. I don't know how sleepy he'll be, but I understand. If you have any other questions, please don't hesitate to ask."

Vaughn and I glanced at one another, and then he said, "Thank you again, Doctor."

After the doctor left the room, I went into Vaughn's arms and hung on tight. "It must've been horrible for you."

Vaughn ran his fingers through his hair. "Everything

happened so fast, I did the best I could to save the boat and us, but, obviously, it wasn't good enough."

"What about getting the boat back to Sabal?" I asked him.

"Let's see how Clint is doing. If he's ready to leave the hospital tomorrow, perhaps Nell can drive him to Sabal, and you and I can sail the boat back. Would you be up for doing that?"

"Sure. I'll call Liana to come and help us. Stephanie and Randolph are staying with the kids now."

"Once I've seen Clint, I'm going to go back to the sailboat to secure it. Someone is watching it now. We'll stay at a hotel nearby."

"Nell and I came prepared to spend the night," I said.

When I saw Clint lying in the hospital bed hooked up to machinery, tears stung my eyes. He looked young and vulnerable, unlike the big executive he liked to project to everyone. Nell was sitting in a chair by his side, holding his hand the best she could.

"Hi," I said softly to him, bending down to kiss his cheek. "You gave us a scare."

"I'm not sure exactly what happened except I saw a speedboat heading right for us," he said weakly.

"Hey, sport," said Vaughn, placing a gentle hand on Clint's head. "How're you doing?"

"Okay, I guess," Clint said. His eyes fluttered closed.

"Vaughn and I are going to secure the sailboat and get his things," I told Nell. "We'll make hotel reservations for tonight, and I'll see to making the arrangements for Liana to take care of the kids."

"Okay," she said. "I'm staying right here for as long as they let me. I'll be in touch."

Vaughn and I hugged her and left.

Back at the boat, we checked in with the dock master to alert him to our situation. Vaughn and I took care of the sails, put away food, and tidied up. We had enough food, water, and drinks for a sail back home.

We locked up the boat again and called a hotel near the hospital for reservations. Then, we headed back to the hotel in an Uber.

"There's a highly rated seafood restaurant near the hospital," said Vaughn. "Let's have Nell meet us there. I want a hot meal. I'm exhausted."

"I bet Nell is as ready as I am for some food and a glass of wine."

"Okay, I'll call her." Vaughn talked to her, and the Uber driver dropped us off at the restaurant.

"How's Clint?" I asked Vaughn before we went inside.

"Nell said he's drowsy and remembers little except the speedboat and being in the water. She doesn't think he realizes the extent of his injuries. And she's delighted we're here at the restaurant. She'll be on her way as soon as possible."

The *Sea Urchin* was a lovely, understated restaurant with an upscale menu. We walked past carved wooden doors into a reception area and were greeted by a hostess wearing black pants and a turquoise knit top.

We were led to a booth with beige leather seats. They softened the deep turquoise color of the walls.

Above the polished wooden table, a dome-shaped turquoise glass lamp hung. Interior lines on the inside of the glass gave an impression of a jellyfish's tentacles, which I found fascinating.

"Your waiter will be right with you," the waitress said.

Minutes later, a man who appeared to be about the same age as Clint, who was in his early forties, walked over to our table.

"My name is Ricardo. I will be serving you tonight. In addition to our regular water, I'm offering still water and bubbly water. What would you like?"

"I'd like still water," I said, knowing I didn't need anything to rile up my nervous stomach.

"I'll have the same," said Vaughn. "And I'd like to look at the wine menu. We have someone joining us."

Vaughn and I sat quietly while the waiter left and returned with a large bottle of cold water and a wine list. "Our wine steward will be right over to help you with a selection." He handed out three menus and left again.

I lingered, looking through the menu. I hadn't realized how hungry I was.

Nell joined us, and our attention turned to her.

"How's Clint? You told your dad you didn't think he realized how hurt he'd been," I said to her.

"He was in a very foggy state," said Nell. "He's on painkillers now, but they'll be careful about keeping him on them for too long. He held my hand and kept saying, "I'm sorry."

"It's not his fault," I said.

"I think he was saying he was sorry for the way he's been treating me," said Nell, unable to hold back tears.

"I see," I said. "You and he will now be able to discuss the situation. I can't imagine he'll be able to return to work for a while."

"Not for a few weeks anyway," said Nell. "It's what I wanted all along, but not like this."

"It's all going to work out for the best," Vaughn said, smiling across the table at her. "Let's try to relax, have a nice dinner, and get to bed early."

"I don't know which I want more right now," said Nell, trying to inject her usual humor into the situation.

"We've got time for it all," I said, reaching to give her hand a reassuring squeeze.

The wine steward approached the table, and he and Vaughn quickly selected a Pinot Noir that would pair well with seafood.

As we sipped our wine, I thought of the past few days and how quickly everything could change. I remembered Nell and Clint's wedding and how they'd made such a sweet, loving couple.

"What is everyone going to order?" asked our waiter. He turned to me.

"I'm going to have the parmesan sole with a lemon-garlic butter sauce," I said.

"I'll have the Chilean Sea Bass," said Nell. "My favorite restaurant at home serves it, and it's delicious."

"And I'm going for the scallops," said Vaughn.

After the waiter had left with our orders, Vaughn glanced at Nell and me. "Ah, it's great to be with two of my favorite people. I'm sorry the circumstances aren't better, but after the scare we had, I'm just glad to be here."

"Did anything happen to *Zephyr*?" Nell asked him.

"No, but I thought it was going to be hit for sure." As one of the Coast Guard told us, after picking up a load of drugs from either an airdrop or from a ship in harbor, these smugglers take off with no regard for anyone else. We were just lucky the Coast Guard boat stopped when they saw us in trouble."

"Shouldn't the smugglers be liable for this?" asked Nell.

"I don't see how anything could be proven, especially without arresting the smugglers," Vaughn said. "It was just a freakish accident."

"And how," I said. "It's hard to believe something like this could happen. But we'll have to deal with the consequences."

Our dinners came, and we dug into the food, exclaiming over the delicious tastes.

As soon as our dirty dishes were cleared away, I felt my eyelids droop and couldn't wait to get to our hotel room for a good sleep. Thank heavens we were close enough to walk to it.

In our hotel room, I called to make sure the kids were okay. Liana assured me everyone was fine there. Satisfied, I brushed my teeth, undressed, and crawled into bed, pleased I'd thought to pack an overnight bag.

Vaughn's arm wrapped around me as he snuggled up against me, and I closed my eyes.

CHAPTER TEN

THE NEXT MORNING, AFTER A QUICK BREAKFAST, THE three of us took an Uber to the hospital, anxious to see Clint.

We loaded my car, still parked in a parking garage, with our luggage, and then headed inside to see Clint.

Catching sight of us, Clint's face twisted with emotion.

Nell rushed to him and awkwardly threw her arms around him, careful not to hurt him.

After she pulled away, Vaughn and I took turns greeting him.

"We're just relieved you're going to be all right. You gave me a scare, buddy," said Vaughn.

I kissed Clint on the cheek. "You've had a bad break. I'm sorry. It's not a pun. As Vaughn said, we're glad you're going to be all right."

Clint grimaced. "It hurts like hell. But I've got to get back to work."

Dr. Taunton came into the room. "I heard that. And I'm afraid you're going to have to take some time off to begin the healing process properly. It will be several weeks before you can begin physical therapy in earnest, but someone from that department will meet with you this morning to review some routines with you. We want to keep you healthy and on the road to recovery."

Clint shook his head. "I was supposed to go back to D. C. this morning." He looked at Nell. "You'll have to call Claudine and tell her what happened. I'll talk to her after I get to Sabal."

"No problem," said Nell. "Where's your phone?"

"I've got it," said Vaughn. He handed it to her.

Nell went out into the hall to call Claudine.

Wanting to be sure she'd be fine, I followed her.

Nell punched in the number and waited.

I watched her face as her eyes widened and her cheeks flushed with color. "No, this isn't Clint. This is Nell, his wife. I'm calling to say that Clint has been involved in an accident and is in the hospital in Tampa with two broken arms. He won't be able to make the flight to D. C. today. He'll call you in a day or two to provide more details."

Nell listened and then said in a firm voice, "No, flying to Tampa to see him isn't necessary. As I said, he'll be in touch as soon as he's able. Goodbye."

After Nell ended the call, she stood a moment, clutching the phone. She looked at me and said, "Claudine is like a viper wrapped around him. She wanted to fly to Tampa to see him, 'the poor baby'. I didn't tell her we were leaving for Sabal as soon as possible."

"I think you're wise to be careful with her," I said, unwilling to tell Nell how unhappy I was seeing Clint with Claudine. She'd attached herself to Clint, taking his arm and smiling up at him. It was clear she wanted more than a professional relationship with him.

A therapist from a team working with the Orthopedic Unit appeared, ending our conversation. Nell followed her inside the room to learn what she had to say.

Vaughn came into the hallway. "Let's leave for the boat as soon as we can."

I went to say goodbye to Nell and Clint and handed the keys to my car to Nell. "Dad and I are headed to the boat. We're going to be sailing her back to Sabal. We'll stay close to shore so we can receive phone calls."

"Thanks. As soon as they allow Clint to leave, I'll drive him home," said Nell. "He's anxious to be out of the hospital."

I hugged Nell and waved to Clint, who was talking with the therapist.

Vaughn and I took an Uber back to the boat.

After attending to business with the harbor master and checking in with the Coast Guard contact, Vaughn and I boarded the boat and made sure we had everything we needed. Vaughn bought some ice and snacks. But with food left over from yesterday's sail, we didn't need much.

Vaughn got behind the wheel, started the engine, and I tossed the deck lines onto the boat and climbed aboard.

As we motored out to where we could set sail, I sighed with relief that no damage had been done to the boat. *Zephyr* was Vaughn's pride and joy, and even though the idea that she'd always be part of the accident with Clint was chilling, we wanted to keep her for a long time.

When we were far enough away from the harbor to have clear sailing, Vaughn asked me to take the wheel while he hoisted the mainsail, then raised the jib.

The wind quickly caught the sails, and we moved forward.

Steering the boat, I couldn't help smiling. There was something special about being under sail. Sea breezes brushed my cheeks, and I inhaled the salty tang of the air.

Vaughn came into the cockpit and stretched his legs out, staring back at me. "There's something about watching you at the wheel that gives me pleasure. Maybe it's the smile on your face. It reminds me that we haven't had the chance to sail alone for some time."

"Robbie loves being on the boat. It's practice for him to be in charge, I'd hate to take that away from him."

"I get it, but that doesn't mean I want to give up on just the two of us being on the boat," said Vaughn.

"It's special," I agreed. "Why don't you take the wheel? I need to call Rhonda to let her know what's happening today. We have a small engagement dinner at the hotel, which I won't be able to make."

I rose, and Vaughn slid behind the wheel.

I went below out of the wind, picked up my cell phone, and punched in Rhonda's number. She answered right away. "Hi, Ann. How's Clint?"

"I think it's going to be a tough day for him. I don't think he or any of us realizes how these fractures might affect him. Nell thinks he is unaware of the extent of his injuries. A woman from the physical therapy unit visited him this morning to discuss home care. Nell was hoping to leave the hospital for Sabal as soon as possible. I've left my car so she can drive Clint home. Vaughn and I are sailing the boat back to Sabal now, so I won't be able to supervise the engagement luncheon."

"No problem. We'll handle it. It looks like a stormy day," Rhonda said, sounding very worried.

"We checked the weather carefully. It's gray and a bit windy, but nothing we can't handle."

"Call me as soon as you arrive in Sabal. I need to know you're safe," said Rhonda.

"Yes, mother," I teased and then felt my eyes filling. Rhonda was mother, daughter, and sister to me.

I ended the call and climbed the stairs to the cockpit. The boat was heeling quite a bit in the wind.

"After the day I had yesterday, I think we both need to put on life jackets," said Vaughn. "No need to zip them closed, but having your arms looped through one will make me feel better."

I retrieved the life jackets, put mine on, and handed Vaughn his. "Thanks," said Vaughn. "Yesterday, I'm not sure what would've happened to Clint if we hadn't had help. By the time I could've turned the boat around and returned to him, he might not have been able to stay afloat. Not with his broken arms."

I gave him a sympathetic look. "It's not your fault it happened. It was just a crazy accident. Who would've guessed to watch out for drug smugglers?"

"I know. My reaction was normal, and it may have even prevented the other boat from hitting us. There was nothing else I could do."

"Then don't blame yourself," I said, sliding behind the wheel next to him and patting his back.

He squeezed my hand. "I guess I needed to hear that."

I leaned my head on his shoulder for a moment, and we continued to let the wind move us along.

Early the next day, we motored into our lagoon and tied the boat up at the dock. Robbie met us to help wash down the boat.

"What happened yesterday?" Robbie asked his dad.

I left them to carry leftover food items up to the house. Liana and the kids were inside the kitchen making tacos for a late lunch.

"Hi, Gammy," said Bailey, running to me. I set the bag of food on the counter and gave her a big hug, and smiled at Liana. "What would we do without you? You've been great about giving us this much time."

"Not a problem," said Liana cheerfully. "Classes are closed for the weekend."

"I want a hug," said Ned, reaching his arms up to me.

I put down Bailey and lifted Ned into my arms, remembering it hadn't been long ago that a boy I hugged this size was Robbie.

"When are Mommy and Daddy coming here?" asked Bailey.

I lowered Ned to the floor and gave each of them a steady look. "They should be here soon. Both of Daddy's arms have been hurt, and he had to stay an extra day. You'll have to be very careful not to bump into him."

"Liana helped us make pictures for him," said Bailey.

I mouthed "thank you" to Liana and said, "While you kids eat, I'll put this food away." It would be essential to keep the kids' routines as simple and easy as possible to minimize meltdowns when Clint was trying to recover.

Robbie and Vaughn came inside, and after the kids had greeted them, Robbie and the little ones settled down to eat.

I went into my bedroom to take a shower and change out of my clothes.

Vaughn came into our bedroom and said, "I'm going to rest for a while."

I kissed him. "You deserve it. It's been a couple of hard days."

l went to shower.

When I came out of the bathroom, Vaughn was lying on the bed snoring softly.

I studied him. He was such a decent man. I knew how upset he was to think he was the person responsible for Clint's injuries.

Not wanting to wake him, I tiptoed out of the room and went to talk to Liana.

We were still chatting on the lanai, sipping lemonade, when Nell called to say they were approaching the neighborhood.

Robbie, Bailey, and Ned joined me in the driveway, and we waited to greet them.

"Remember what I told you about not bumping into Daddy," I said as Nell pulled the car into the driveway.

I hurried to open the door for Clint while Nell went to greet the children.

Clint grimaced as he turned to get out of the car. "I need to take more medicine."

I saw him struggle to smile as the kids stood by me, saying, "Hi, Daddy!"

With both arms in slings, I helped him steady himself on his feet. "Hi, Bailey, hi, Ned," he managed to say, though I knew it cost him to hold back a groan.

Nell rushed to Clint's side and put her arm around his shoulders. "Let's get you inside."

"Your room is ready for you," I said. "The lounge chair there might be more comfortable for you than on the bed, even though the mattress is adjustable."

"Thanks," he murmured. "I need to lie down. Either place will do."

Nell turned to me. "Ann, if you keep track of the kids now, I'll let them speak to their father later."

"Will do," I said. "We can go for a swim, and then we can watch a television program."

Vaughn appeared. "Need another steadying hand?"

"Yes," said Nell. "I'll run ahead and get the room ready."

The kids and I followed behind as Vaughn led Clint into the house and to the guestroom he was sharing with Nell.

"Okay. Dad will see you later," I told Bailey and Ned. "How about us having a swim in the pool?" The gray skies of the morning had given way to a sunny afternoon.

The worried looks on their faces were replaced with excitement, and I helped them get into their bathing suits.

Robbie went next door to be with his best friend, Brett. Liana left for the day but promised to be on standby if we needed her.

Later, Nell and Vaughn joined the kids and me at the pool.

The accident had taken a toll on us all.

After playing in the pool with the kids, Vaughn and I

settled in front of the television on the lanai to watch a kids' television show with them while Nell went to check on Clint and get some rest for herself.

"How much help do you think Clint will need for daily activities?" I asked Vaughn after the kids had decided to work with their new Lego sets.

"He was able to take his right arm out of the sling to use the bathroom," Vaughn said. "That arm has a splint on it. That's a big relief for him. But he'll need help in many other ways. It's smart for Nell to push the idea of the family staying here, where he and the kids can be looked after."

"I think it would be selfish of him to ask Nell to go back to D.C., where neither she nor the kids would have the support they have here," I said.

"Agreed," said Vaughn. "But they have to work it out for themselves. He's worried about the project he's working on."

"Nell was upset about the phone call with Claudine. Claudine is one pushy lady."

They'll work it out," said Vaughn. "But I'm concerned that Clint has this idea he needs to make a lot more money in order to make Nell happy. She's told me she doesn't know why he feels that way except that he knows I'm financially secure. She's tried to explain that she needs his presence, not his money."

"We're both successful, and I believe he feels he has to measure up. He took this new job to prove himself."

Vaughn shook his head. "Nell is a sensible person who was raised to believe that you don't judge a person by how much money he or she has."

Nell walked into the room and plopped down on a chair next to the couch. "Clint is sleeping peacefully."

"How about you? Did you get any rest?" I asked her.

"No, my mind is spinning. You don't object to having us here, do you? Clint will need lots of help. And I still want to work at the hotel like we planned."

"You can stay for as long as you want," I said.

"Yes," said Vaughn. "There's plenty of room and lots of help available. It's what you planned all along."

"But Clint is worried about completing the project he's working on," said Nell. "I told him that he's not going back to D.C. until after his first post-op appointment, and that I needed him here with me and the kids. We didn't resolve that issue, but at least we know where we stand on it."

Nell's cell phone rang. She looked at it and rose. "That's Clint buzzing me for help."

After she left, I said to Vaughn. "This is one time I'm going to defend Nell. It's crazy to think she doesn't need support, too."

Vaughn patted my back. "We just need everything to settle down."

A short while later, Nell walked onto the lanai, her face an ugly red.

I got to my feet. "Nell, what's wrong?"

"It's Claudine. She called Clint's cell while I was with him. She's suggesting that Clint fly to D.C. tomorrow. She said he could stay with her where she has help. I told her that Clint was staying right here with my family. Then she suggested she come stay at the hotel, allowing Clint and her to work in Sabal. I told her that Clint wouldn't be working for a few days, as per the doctor's orders. Now, both she and Clint are mad at me."

"Let me go talk to Clint," I said, being careful not to show how angry I was.

Nell shrugged. "Fat good it will do. But, sure, go ahead and try to talk some sense into him."

CHAPTER ELEVEN

I FOUND CLINT LYING IN THE LOUNGE CHAIR, HIS EYES closed, both of his arms in slings. Seeing him in this vulnerable position, I wondered what had happened to the son-in-law I loved and admired that had led him to change his ways. He'd been ambitious but down-to-earth. Nell mentioned that the partners in the company had many more benefits and perks and were more successful. Had he decided he wanted that too? For Nell?

He opened his eyes.

I took a seat on the bed nearby and sat facing him. "Nell's upset about your decision to fly to D.C., and I'm concerned that Claudine is apparently pressuring you to disregard the doctor's orders to work with her."

"Claudine told me the group hired me specifically for this project, and if I don't follow through and get this done, I may lose not only my equity in it, but my job."

Frowning, I leaned forward and patted his hand. "Clint, it doesn't make sense for you to go to D.C.. First of all, with your injuries, you're not close to functioning at peak performance. Secondly, this is a holiday weekend. Are all the people expected to work this weekend?"

Clint shook his head. "No. A lot of them went away. But they weren't tied to this project."

"Then why is Claudine insistent on working with you this weekend?"

"She bought into the equity of this project like I did, with a lot more money. She doesn't want to lose it because of timing."

"It doesn't add up to me. Deals don't always work on a specific timeline. Lots of circumstances can change that. This should be one of them," I said.

"Ann, I can't afford to lose the money either. I knew it was a risky deal, but that's how you make big money. You take a risk and make it work in order to cash in."

I studied him and let out a long breath. "What made you decide to do this? You've bought into the concept of projecting a very successful lifestyle with a private school for the kids, fancy cars, and a membership to a pricey golf club. That doesn't seem like you."

"I know. But that was part of the deal. If you look successful, you're more likely to be successful. I'm sorry about that concept because it's so much pressure to keep everything going."

"Whenever you want to pull the plug, you have my support. Vaughn's too, I'm sure."

"That's just it. I want to provide my wife with a wonderful life without needing the support of her parents," said Clint.

"You provide Nell and the kids by being there for them in person, loving and supporting them. You're a very bright man, Clint. You don't need to have a lot of money to make them happy."

Clint stared out the window.

"And another thing. I saw the way Claudine was with you. Her intentions are very obvious, and you didn't seem to be fighting her off. If you ever hurt Nell and destroy your marriage, you'll have a line of people waiting to get back at you. I'll be the first one there."

His eyes widened, and then he nodded. "No worries."

I got to my feet and faced him. "I love you, Clint. I want what's best for you. You and your family."

"I know," he said, giving me a glum look.

I left the room and went back to the lanai.

"Well, what did he say?" asked Nell. "Is he going to stay here?"

"I don't know about that," I said. "But I have the feeling Clint is beginning to see that the golden handcuffs his business has given him might not be what he wants after all."

"That sounds promising," said Vaughn.

"He never said exactly that, but he's worried. He and Claudine each stand to lose a lot of money if their deal doesn't work."

"That's exactly why I was hesitant to have him buy into the deal. It sounded risky to me, but he seemed so sure it would be a wise move for us," said Nell.

"He believes he's done it for all the right reasons," I said.

"What if Claudine comes to Sabal to stay in the hotel?" Nell asked.

"There's nothing we can do about that," I said. "We'll take it one step at a time."

Nell sighed and shook her head.

The next morning, I went to the hotel alone. Nell stayed behind to make sure Clint was doing as well as could be expected. The first few days following surgery were typically the most challenging.

I stopped in the kitchen to get a cup of coffee.

Consuela came right over to me. "How's Clint?"

"He'll be fine, but it's going to be difficult," I said. "He was hurt pretty bad."

Consuela sighed and shook her head. "Such a shame. How will he be able to work? Is he going to stay in Sabal for a while? Nell told me he had to go right back to D.C."

"It's something Nell and Clint are trying to figure out. Frankly, I'm concerned. I think he should stay here for at least a couple of weeks until his body begins to recover."

"I'll make his favorite egg casserole and send it home with

you," Consuela said.

I hugged her. "Thanks."

I left the kitchen and went to my office to see how procedures had been handled over the weekend. Rhonda looked up at me from her desk. "Who's Claudine Everett?"

A lump settled in the pit of my stomach. "A business partner of Clint's. Why?"

"Apparently, she made a fuss checking in last night. She wanted the Presidential Suite. For a deep discount."

I sighed, lowered myself into my chair, and faced Rhonda. "Remember how I told you there was something about Claudine that I didn't like or trust? This behavior is an example of why I feel that way. Is she in the Presidential Suite?"

"No," said Rhonda. "Bernie said no. Not at that price."

"Bless him," I said. "Clint was supposed to fly to D.C. with Claudine in the company's private jet yesterday. When Nell called to cancel the trip, she was very specific about Clint needing to rest as the doctor ordered. Now, it's clear that Claudine is going to ignore that."

"What's the rush?" asked Rhonda.

"The timing of putting this deal together appears to be crucial. Clint is worried that he and Claudine will lose a lot of money if they can't pull it off." I couldn't help feeling anxious.

Rhonda gave me a thoughtful look. "Will could have been involved in many big-ticket deals with major companies, but he has always maintained that he's happier with his own success, providing clients with excellent information."

"Claudine may have checked into the hotel, but I'm uncomfortable about her being at my house. She practically ordered me to make sure Vaughn, not I, drop Clint off for the flight to D.C. She told Clint she was disappointed not to meet one of her favorite stars. I don't want someone like that in my home."

"I don't blame you," said Rhonda. "That kind of intrusion could be a problem."

"I'm going to call Nell now and tell her my feelings," I said, taking a sip of coffee before punching in her number.

When Nell picked up my call, I told her I didn't want Claudine at the house and waited for a response.

"I needed to know you feel that way because she's already phoned Clint. I didn't pick up the call because Clint was sleeping. But eventually, I'll have to talk to her and make that clear."

"Thanks," I said. "There's something off about Claudine. As far as I'm concerned, Clint can do what he needs to at the house, including setting up an office. But I don't want them working together there."

"And I want them to wait until Clint gets stabilized," said Nell. "He's on pretty strong pain killers now, which means he won't be at his best to work anyway."

"I'm glad we agree on this. Stars like Vaughn have to be very careful about overzealous fans. That's one reason we live in a gated community."

"I agree," said Nell. " I wouldn't want anything to happen to Daddy or you because of someone like her." I could hear frustration in her voice.

"Thanks for understanding." I ended the call and turned to Rhonda. "Hopefully, that will take care of any intrusion into our privacy."

"You told me you were afraid that Claudine and Clint might be having an affair," said Rhonda. "If so, Claudine isn't simply going to walk away."

"Especially someone as aggressive as she is," I said. "Now, tell me about the goings on at the hotel. How was the engagement dinner?"

Rhonda lifted her coffee cup in a salute. "It turned out to be a goldmine for us. The hostess is none other than the sister of our governor, and the three other women present with their husbands have decided to book family weddings with us."

"Thanks for handling that. I assume Annette was there to assist you," I said.

"Yes, and you know how well she connects with people. She was able to say that she was one of our wedding coordinators. That worked well for us."

"Well done!" I gave Rhonda a high five. We celebrated the big occasions at the hotel, but we also celebrated smaller ones. You never knew when a seemingly simple event would help bring in future business.

We were going over the financials for the previous day when someone tapped at the door, and then it flew open.

Surprised, Rhonda and I stopped talking and looked up to see Claudine.

I got to my feet. "Claudine, is there something we can help you with?"

She narrowed her eyes at me. "You can help me have a meeting with Clint. I'm his partner and deserve to have some time with him. His wife tells me I'm not welcome at your house. Is that true?"

I drew a deep breath. "My home is a private space for Vaughn and me. Though you can't meet Clint there, I think he should be able to talk to you on the phone. But he's pretty drugged up at the moment and under the doctor's order to rest for a few days. He has been through a lot of traumatic experiences. I would think you'd honor that information."

Claudine drew a deep breath and studied me. "Did you know that Clint was considering leaving his wife? He and I had an understanding."

I gripped the edge of my desk. "I find that hard to believe. But really, it has nothing to do with Clint getting better. As I said, you're welcome to call him. And he can decide if, when, and where, other than my house, he can meet with you."

Rhonda stood and put an arm around my shoulder. "Miss, Claudine, is it? You're upsetting my business partner, and I won't allow that. Your business with Clint Dawson is not ours. You'd better take a hike."

Claudine glared at Rhonda, then whipped around and left the room, slamming the door behind her.

"Wow!" said Rhonda. "She really is a bitch. Are you okay, Annie?"

I nodded, but inside, I was trembling with rage. I thought about calling Nell and decided not to. She'd have to handle the situation on her own.

That night, when I got home, Robbie was with the kids on the lanai while Vaughn was seasoning the filet mignons he was going to grill for dinner.

"Hi, darling. How are you?" Vaughn asked me.

"It's been quite a day. Where are Nell and Clint?"

Vaughn indicated the guest wing of the house. "When I last checked, both of them were napping."

"Claudine came into the office and demanded to meet with Clint. She wanted to know if it was true that she wasn't allowed to visit him at our house. I told her, yes, that it was our private space for obvious reasons. I suggested she call Clint, and he could decide how to best proceed." I sighed. "She also told me that Clint was going to leave Nell, that she and Clint had what she called an arrangement."

Vaughn's eyebrows shot up. "Really? I don't believe that. Not after the talks I had with Clint on the boat. What's Claudine's game?"

"I don't know, but I don't trust her. Something weird is going on. Something that doesn't make sense."

Nell padded into the kitchen. "I thought I heard voices. How are things at the hotel, Ann?"

"That engagement dinner last night brought us the

possibility of many new weddings. And the high tea the other day went well enough that we're considering offering it as a Christmas gift for some of the locals to purchase. Sunday afternoon teas will be served throughout the high season.

"I loved seeing how the teas are set up. I can't wait to participate in them," said Nell.

"Have you and Clint talked about his staying here?" I asked. It would make a difference if Nell couldn't work at the hotel.

"Clint has agreed to stay here for a few days as the doctor has requested," said Nell. "Then he hopes to go to D.C. to work on his deal. He's talking about leaving the company, but he's worried about getting his share of equity money back."

"How will he handle traveling? He'll still need help," I said.

"He's asked me to go with him. I told him I'll do it on the condition he promises to return to Sabal as quickly as possible." Nell looked down at the floor and shuffled her feet. When she looked up, her eyes were full of tears. "He told me that Claudine thinks he's going to leave me, but that it isn't true. He told her so. As the daughter of one of the business owners, she believes she can choose any man in the company she wants and is willing to strong-arm them into a romantic relationship. She tried that with another man who has since left the firm."

I leaned against the kitchen counter and let out a loud huff of breath. "What a mess."

Nell studied me. "As Rhonda would say, a freakin' mess."

CHAPTER TWELVE

I DECIDED TO SPEAK TO CLINT ABOUT MY CONVERSATION with Claudine. I wanted him to understand the importance of not having her in my home. but that I'd help him in any other way that I could.

Ever since Nell brought him home to meet the family, Clint and I had grown fond of one another. I liked his ambition to work hard and succeed, but somewhere along the line, it had turned into something different. His goal had become a need to have more material things as a way to prove to himself and others that he could provide for Nell as well as her father could. The mistake in all this was that Nell wasn't materialistic. She was just as content with her old car and her first house as it was. What she wanted was to be with him.

When I walked into the guest room, Clint was standing by the open sliding door leading to a private deck.

"Hi," I said softly, not wanting to scare him.

He turned around and smiled at me. "This is such a beautiful spot. And quiet."

"Our home and our privacy are very important to Vaughn and me. I hope you understand why someone like Claudine isn't welcome here. She's already expressed her curiosity about Vaughn. We must have a place where we're safe from prying eyes."

"I get it. I really do. Nell feels the same way," said Clint.

"That being said, we have no problem with your setting up a Zoom call in any part of the house. Somewhere comfortable for you," I said. "We can help you."

"I think that might be best," Clint admitted. "Nell and I talked about going back to D.C. so I could work on the plan, but I've reconsidered. Claudine and I can work on it together online. I want to get back to playing with the kids and my other activities."

"Well, then, let us know when and where you want to set up the meetings, and Nell and I will help you feel at ease. Vaughn is home for a while. He can help too."

"I haven't felt up to it, but I'm sure I'll be able to work tomorrow," said Clint. "I can do some number crunching with my right hand. Thank God that arm is in better shape than my left one."

"Is there anything I can do for you now?" I asked.

Clint studied me and then spoke. "I told Nell that Claudine thinks I'm going to divorce her. But I'm not."

"I appreciate that you brought that up. Claudine told me the same thing. Why would she say that?"

Clint looked uncomfortable, but he kept a steady stare at me. "For a while, I was flattered by Claudine's attention. At home, Nell was preoccupied with the children, upset with me for taking the job with Everett, Shuster, and Donnelly in the first place, and was angry about the additional hours I spent working. And then with the equity money in balance I had to increase time and energy on the project."

I wondered if I should say anything and then decided I owed it to both Nell and Clint to speak up. "Remember, I saw you with Claudine. And I didn't like it. Your behavior suggested that you were more than just business partners."

Clint's eyes widened. "But that's all it is. I swear. You know how much I love Nell. More than that, we've promised never to hurt each other."

"But you've been ignoring your family while spending hours with Claudine. What's that all about? It's just a work project. It may be an important one, but your family needs to come first. Claudine is acting as if you're courting her. It's a problem. Don't diminish what you've done. You need to have a talk with Claudine and set her straight. You'd better take care of that now. Am I clear?"

"Yes," said Clint.

I'd heard enough bullshit from my ex to realize Clint was telling the truth. His cheeks were flushed, his eyes wet. But there was a steadiness to his gaze that I admired.

"Okay, then. Let's work together as a family to support your marriage. Nell mentioned Claudine had played a similar game for another man's attention in the firm."

"Yes. He left the firm because of it," said Clint. "I understand that better now."

"Hanky-panky between co-workers is nothing new," I said. "It's a relief to know that in this case, it's not going to work. But it does make me see that you and Nell need to spend more time together."

"Even if she's going to continue to work at the hotel?" said Clint. "How?"

"That's between you and her," I said. "But it's something you should discuss. Maybe being a mother doesn't have to mean giving up what you love doing. In Nell's case, she loves being involved in activities outside the home, in addition to caring for her children and husband. And we both know how much she's wanted to move here. In fact, at one point, she told me you were almost ready to do so."

Clint eased himself onto the lounge chair. "I realize I haven't been entirely fair to her and the kids. But I thought I was doing it for them. I still do. Let me get past this project, and then Nell and I will make some decisions."

"I'm proud of you, Clint, for being so honest with me." I leaned down and kissed his cheek.

"Thanks for not judging me too harshly for allowing the situation with Claudine to get out of hand. I love Nell and will do whatever I can to save our marriage," he said, closing his eyes and lying back against the chair.

The next morning, Nell and I prepared the library for the Zoom call between Claudine and Clint. We had a notebook and pen lying beside his laptop on top of Vaughn's desk, a pitcher of ice water within reach, and a calculator lying close by.

Clint sat in the desk chair and surveyed the room with satisfaction. "Nell, you sit over there and take notes. I want to have a witness to conversations between Claudine and me. She told me she's reworked the numbers, and I'm not sure I'll agree to them. That wasn't part of the deal."

"How will she feel about me being part of this?" Nell asked.

"She has no choice. I'll record our conversation as well," said Clint. "I've done a lot of thinking about this and many other things."

"Okay. You know I'll help you," said Nell, leaning down and kissing his cheek.

"I'll see you later. I've got to get to the hotel," I said. "But if you need me for anything, let me know. Liana is here for the children. And Vaughn will be coming and going."

Nell and Clint smiled and waved, and I left the room. Robbie was back in school, and Vaughn had left for a theater meeting.

I hugged and kissed Bailey and Ned, waved to Liana, and headed toward the hotel feeling better about Nell and Clint. They'd always worked together as a team. This would help heal the hurt and disappointments of the past.

A little while later, I was unprepared for a frantic phone call from Nell as I sat with Rhonda in our office. Trying to remain calm, Nell said, "Claudine refused to let me help Clint.

She said any meeting should be here at the house with him, not me. Clint finally agreed for me to leave the room after I turned on Vaughn's tape recorder. I get the feeling she's up to something not quite right with this business project. Apparently, the numbers she and Clint came up with for the sale of the property did not meet with approval from the board."

"That shouldn't be a cause for alarm," I said. "Financial deals take time and a lot of compromise."

"I don't have all the details, but it involves the sale of one property so it can be re-purchased and then sold as part of a group of properties to another buyer," said Nell.

"No wonder Clint has felt under such pressure," I said. "You've done what you could to help. I'm sure Clint is grateful."

"I'm going to go ahead and register the kids in school. You don't mind my using Liana to babysit until I establish a better order, do you?" asked Nell.

"Not at all. She told me she enjoys your children." I tried to keep my voice neutral, but the possibility of Nell and her family moving here made me want to jump with joy.

We ended the call, and I turned to Rhonda. "Nell was going to take notes for Clint's business call, but Claudine wouldn't allow it."

"What do you know about this person?" Rhonda said, frowning. "Let's look her up."

We checked Claudine Everett online.

She was listed as being 38 years old, married and divorced, the daughter of Louis and Isabelle Everett. An older sister, Natasha, had died as a toddler.

"Look at this," said Rhonda. "Louis Everett's company, Everett, Shuster, and Donnelly Real Estate Enterprises has had trouble with some of its dealings. One court case was recently settled for $10 million."

I shook my head. "Why would Clint get involved with a company like that?"

"They're high rollers," said Rhonda. "You said Clint wanted to prove he could support Nell in style."

"The company recruited him," I said. "He might have been satisfied to go along as he was. Nell and Clint were doing well until this project came up. And then he had the opportunity to share in the equity."

"Clint is bright, attractive, and would be appealing to any company," said Rhonda. "They must have given him an excellent opportunity for him to want to become part of it."

"He placed a second mortgage on their house to buy equity in this special deal," I said. "Nell didn't like the idea, but she went along with it."

"This doesn't sound like Clint," said Rhonda. "It seems a bit risky. Why'd he do it?"

"Like I said, I think he wanted to prove himself to Nell and us." I couldn't help clutching my hands together. Alarm bells were ringing in my head.

"You know that Reggie and Will are willing to help in any way they can," said Rhonda.

"I've kept that thought in the back of my mind. But Vaughn and I decided that though we can show our support, we have to let Nell and Clint work this out on their own."

"Well, I'm just sayin'." Rhonda's voice shook with emotion. "You know I love those kids."

"Thanks. I know you do."

Later that day, after Rhonda left to go to a school event with Angela's children, I was surprised when Nell came into my office.

"Hello, good to see you," I said. "What's going on?"

"I just signed up the kids for school," Nell said. "And I

talked to Annette and Lauren to see about working in the hospitality department."

"You're not going to D.C. with Clint?" I asked her.

She shook her head. "Clint is upset about the new numbers Claudine came up with. He's not going to leave Sabal until this situation is resolved."

"Did you know Everett, Shuster, and Donnelly had to settle a lawsuit for $10 million?" I asked her.

Nell shook her head and plopped down into the chair facing my desk. "I knew that a legal matter had been settled recently, but not for that amount of money. I've never liked the people there."

"Did you tell Clint that?" I asked her, needing to know.

"Yes, I have, but I eventually stopped. The disagreement was ruining our marriage, and I didn't want to do that to the children. They adore their father."

"Does Clint understand that?" I asked.

"He does. We've discussed it as well as several other matters. I've wanted to support Clint, and I've tried to do that. but I can't pretend I think this is a healthy situation."

"If you or Clint need any advice, you know that Reggie and Will would be more than happy to help," I said. "They're family, after all."

"Thanks. Clint is meeting with Reggie tomorrow," Nell said.

"Oh, good," I said. "What can I do to help the kids get ready for school? Why don't we take them shopping for new clothes?"

"I brought some with me, but that would be great. Bailey is very aware of fashion, and it might make it more exciting for her to have a couple of new clothing items to wear. And Ned is growing so fast, he needs a couple, too."

"We'll make it an exciting adventure," I said.

"I'll meet you back home," said Nell. "Thanks, Ann.

You're always sweet and understanding."

"You're my daughter, and I love you," I said, moving close to hug her.

CHAPTER THIRTEEN

LATER THAT DAY, LOADED DOWN WITH PACKAGES, I followed Nell, Bailey, and Ned inside the house. They were eager to show Clint their purchases. It was an enjoyable, practical way to ease the kids into a new school situation. Neither of them would be wearing private school uniforms anymore.

Clint was sitting on the lanai with Vaughn and was being kind about "oohing" and "aahing" over the items Bailey and Ned eagerly showed him.

After the children left the lanai to change into their swimsuits, Clint said, "I'm not sure what's going on with the business project I've been working on, but I'm going to seek some confidential advice from Reggie. It's really important that no one in the company knows I'm doing this."

I exchanged worried looks with Vaughn.

"Believe me, we won't tell," I said. "But I do think it's a wise move on your part. I understand the firm recently made a $10 million settlement on a legal case."

"That happened after I joined the firm. The situation was never mentioned in any due diligence I did on the company," said Clint. "A hush-hush deal for sure."

"How did you do on your Zoom call with Claudine?" I asked.

"She's reworked the numbers, and I don't like them. The numbers she and I had projected didn't satisfy the requirement to cut costs enough. She's suggesting eliminating more employees and paying those who are left less money. I recorded the conversation, and I've printed the financials she provided, but I'm going to need help to review and verify the numbers. My broken arm is giving me fits if I work for any length of time."

"Is that what you're using Reggie for?" I asked him.

Clint nodded. "I can't leave it to Claudine to put together a new plan that I can agree to. Her father would, I'm sure, applaud her for cutting the costs of the deal, but that's not what I agreed to when I signed on."

Clint's cell rang. He picked up the call.

I watched his face as he listened. His eyes widened, and the color left his cheeks.

"I see. Was any damage done to the rest of the house? I'm recovering from an accident in Florida, but I'll have our insurance company come in to assess the situation. Yes. you can reach me at this number."

"What's wrong?" asked Nell, coming to his side.

"That was the police department. There's been a break-in at the house," said Clint. "It was discovered by Libby, our next-door neighbor, when she came into the house to water the plants. They said my office has been turned upside down, but the rest of the house has hardly been touched. It obviously has something to do with work. Thank God, I have my computer and any backup information with me here."

"Oh, my God! That's terrible. What if the children or I had been in the house?" said Nell. "I'll call Libby now." Nell's cell rang. "Oh, here she is calling me."

"Hi, Libby," said Nell. "The police have just notified Clint of the break-in. What can you tell me?"

Clint signaled Nell.

"Libby, I'm going to put you on speakerphone so Clint and my parents can hear," said Nell. "Do you mind?"

"Not at all," Libby said. "I don't know what the police told you, but when I went into the house to water the plants, I didn't notice anything out of the ordinary. Not until I got to Clint's office. Papers were everywhere, desk drawers were open, and items were scattered throughout the office closet."

"Did you check the rest of the house?" Nell asked her.

"Not until the police arrived," said Nell. "They made certain there was no one inside and then allowed me to make sure the upstairs rooms were okay."

"There was no other sign of things not being right?" asked Clint. "What about the alarm?"

"For some reason, the alarm didn't go off," said Libby. "I think it's been broken. But you'll have to check with the police about that."

"Sounds like professionals," Vaughn said quietly, and I silently agreed.

"Thank you, Libby. I'm grateful you weren't hurt, that whoever it was had already gone," said Nell. "We'll hire a security company to patrol the house, and I'll fly up to D.C. to take care of this. Clint is recovering from a fall and has two broken arms."

"Oh, no! That's awful. I hope he heals quickly," said Libby.

"One last question," said Clint. "Did you hear or see anything related to the break-in?"

"No," said Libby. "I was away for most of the day volunteering at the hospital. I came over to your house after I got home."

"I'll let you know my plans," said Nell. "Thanks again."

After Nell ended the call, the four of us sat quietly. This was no amateur trying to get information. It was a professional who definitely wanted to find material related to Clint's project.

"I don't like the idea of you going alone to the house," said Clint. "Even with added security."

"I'll go with her," I said. "Like you, Clint, I don't want Nell to have to handle the situation alone."

Nell turned to Clint. "I'll pick up some extra things for the kids and us. And I'm going to pack up valuables and bring them here."

"Smart idea," said Clint. "I'm going to remain here for the foreseeable future. It's something you've wanted, and since the accident and now this, it makes sense."

"What about Claudine and your project?" I asked him.

"That will have to be worked on here in Sabal," said Clint.

Vaughn frowned. "We're pretty secure here. Just in case, though, I'll hire a security company to patrol our house."

"I'm sorry it's come to this," said Nell. "If you're uncomfortable with having us here, we can find another place to stay."

"Nell, honey, this is your home," I said. "We can't let others scare us away."

"Right," said Vaughn. "I'll see that you and your family are safe with us."

"It's just information they want," said Clint. "But, Nell, after taking care of this, I'm comforted knowing you're going to be staying in Sabal."

"One day at a time. Are you going to let Claudine know about the break-in?" I asked Clint.

"No," he said with a firmness I understood. "I think they're playing me for a fool. I may have fallen for the glamour of this company, but I'm better than that."

I glanced at Vaughn.

He gave Clint a nod of approval. "I think you are, too."

The next day, Nell and I flew to D.C. and took an Uber to her house in Bethesda, Maryland.

As the driver pulled into the driveway of the two-story luxurious house, I studied it, thinking it looked like many colonial-style homes outside Boston. The exterior was gray-painted clapboard with sparkling white trim. The front entrance door was bright red and was an integral part of the wide front porch.

"It's a pretty house," I commented as Nell and I got out.

"It's too much house for us—six bedrooms and five bathrooms. We don't need all that space. But Clint was right about it being a house designed for a quick resale. It has everything someone could want."

"Are you thinking of selling it?" I asked, surprised.

Nell stood looking at the building and sighed. "The idea of someone breaking into it is creepy. I'm not sure I'll ever feel the same way about this house."

"Well, we've got a lot to do while we're here," I said. "Put me to work."

"I'm meeting with the insurance agent this afternoon. Before then, we need to conduct a thorough survey of the house to make sure nothing is missing. I want to pack the more valuable items and store them in Florida. There's not a lot. It's mostly smaller objects—family jewelry, silver, and the like. Sentimental pieces. I can pack up in the car and drive them to Florida."

"And the children's stuff?" I asked.

"I want to be judicious about what I take to Florida. With Christmas coming up, they'll want a few items from here," said Nell.

I followed her to the front door and waited while she entered the security system's access code.

We waited for a signal that it was unlocked, but it didn't come. Frowning, Nell turned to me. "I guess it hasn't been fixed yet. She took out a key and unlocked the front door with no trouble.

Inside the foyer, we stood a moment while Nell checked the security system keyboard. "It's been disarmed," said Nell.

"I guess the police left it like it was. I'm to call the security company."

"Where do you want me to start?" I asked her.

"Let's do a walk-through of the house. I need to make sure nothing else was touched," said Nell.

We left our purses in the kitchen and walked through the rooms on the first floor, then the second floor, leaving Clint's office to the last.

Nell opened the door, and we peered at the disturbance.

"What a mess," said Nell. She lifted her cell phone and took photos from the doorway, and then we moved inside the room to record the scene with more photographs.

While we were there, Nell called Clint and put him on the speaker. "Ann and I are in your office. We've taken photographs. What else should we do? What would you like us to look for?"

"I want you to go to the closet and see if you can find a key hanging along the side of the wooden trim behind the door. When you find it, I want you to take it to the garage and open a toolbox there."

"Really? Okay. What will I find there?" Nell asked him.

"You'll see," said Clint. "There are personal papers. I put the paperwork in there in case something like this trouble came up. I'll hang on while you search."

Nell found the key, and we went into the garage and looked for a metal toolbox.

We found it under the workbench among some other items. Nell tried the key and unlocked the box.

Inside, several envelopes were marked and sealed.

"Okay," said Clint, "I want you to remove the envelope called 'Employee Agreement'. There should be another marked 'Equity Agreement'. Find the one marked 'pay stubs' and the one marked 'benefits package'. I want you to bring those to Florida when you return."

"Why are they here and not with your other personal papers?" I asked Clint, too curious to let it go.

"The man who left the company due to his relationship with Claudine warned me to be sure to keep all original materials related to my employment with Everett, Shuster, and Donnelly," explained Clint. "When he wanted to get his equity investment back on the project I'm now working on, the company attempted to screw him out of what percentage he was owed, saying he didn't have the proper paperwork to back up his claim."

"Are you leaving the company?" asked Nell.

"I want that option," said Clint. "I'm not sure what's happening. I just know I don't like how the original project agreement is changing."

"Let me know if you need anything else," Nell said. "I'll bring the toolbox with me because I've decided to drive your car to Florida. That way, I can pack what I want to keep safe."

"Okay. Thanks. Do you have hotel reservations for tonight?"

"Yes, but depending on how fast we get packed up, we might not stay nearby. We might get on the road, away from here," said Nell, with such urgency I realized she thought we might be in danger.

A shiver traveled down my spine.

"Keep me informed," said Clint.

"Of course," Nell said. "Love you."

"I love you, too," said Clint.

Nell ended the call and faced me. "Let's work fast, Ann. I don't want to stay here any longer than we have to."

"Okay," I said. "Tell me what you want me to do."

"Will you work in the dining room?" Nell asked me. "There are empty moving boxes here in the garage. I want to pack up the family silver and other items you think I should keep safe. I'm going to box up jewelry and other items from the master bedroom. Then we'll pack the kids' things they might need."

I grabbed some empty boxes and went into the dining room.

Nell came into the room and handed me some plain, packing paper. "This is left over from our move here. It works better than newspapers."

She showed me what she wanted packed, and I set to work while she called the security company.

"I'm cancelling the insurance adjustor," Nell said. "As the police told us, I see no evidence that any other part of the house was disturbed. Just the office."

I went to work packing a lot of the dining room. Many of those items were family pieces that Vaughn's first wife had loved and had been given to Nell.

Later, while the security company worked on the system, I packed up articles from the children's rooms—some clothing, books, and special items like posters, stuffed animals. If Nell and Clint decided to move to Florida, they'd take care of the rest. In the meantime, while Bailey and Ned stayed with Vaughn and me, they'd be more comfortable with familiar items around them.

While I was working in the kitchen, the doorbell rang, and Nell went to answer it.

Libby Tayson from next door entered the house.

"My! What's going on?" Libby asked, gazing at the boxes we'd placed by the door to the garage.

"We're packing up a few items to take to Florida. I'll be staying there until after the New Year. Come meet my mother, Ann Sanders. She and her business partner, Rhonda Grayson, own The Beach House Hotel. Ann, this is Libby Tayson, my best friend and next-door neighbor."

Libby held out her hand. "Nice to meet you. My husband and I are hoping to stay at your hotel sometime this winter. Nell talks about it all the time."

"Be sure to let us know when you'd like to come," I said. "We'll try to accommodate you."

"Thanks." Libby gave Nell a hug. "Are you all right?"

"I should ask you the same," said Nell, standing back and studying Libby. "I'm glad you weren't hurt. You didn't see or hear anyone?"

Libby shook her head. "No, whoever broke in knew exactly where they should go and what they wanted. Did they get away with anything?"

"We're not sure. Clint is still in Florida, where he's recovering from his accident. We're pretty certain the paperwork important to us hasn't been touched."

"What happened to Clint?" asked Libby.

Nell told her about the accident and then said, "For the moment, he's remaining in Florida. We don't know when that will change. It depends on how fast he heals."

"That makes sense," said Libby. "I see the security company is here to fix the system. Do you still want me to water the plants?"

"If you don't mind," said Nell. "But if you're uncomfortable doing it, I'll hire a service."

"I'm happy to do it for you," said Libby.

"Why don't we move the smaller plants into the kitchen to make it easier for you?" I suggested, and both Nell and Libby acknowledged the idea with bright smiles.

"Perfect," said Nell. "Then we'll place the other plants in the sunroom. By the way, I'll send you the new code for the security system via text. Ann and I will be leaving this evening."

"Okay. Again, nice to meet you, Ann," said Libby. "I'd better be on my way."

After she left, I said to Nell, "Libby is a kind friend."

Nell's smile was warm. "Yes. I'll miss her. Even so, Sabal is more like home to me."

"I'm reassured that Clint is keeping his options open," I said, unwilling to put any pressure on Nell to move to Sabal permanently.

CHAPTER FOURTEEN

AFTER MAKING CERTAIN THAT FOOD IN THE KITCHEN WAS either stored properly or discarded, Nell and I took one last walk through the house to make sure we had what we wanted for the drive to Florida. We decided we'd drive straight through because we both needed to be at The Beach House Hotel.

At the last minute, Nell removed two paintings from the wall and loaded a couple of decorative pieces into the car. We agreed that no one would probably return to the house for whatever they were looking for, but it was wise to take some of these items with us, just in case.

We got into Clint's packed Audi A6 and rolled out of the garage.

Before pulling away, Nell stopped the car and studied the house. "It's beautiful, but I never really wanted to move here. We were fine living closer to town in a smaller home. This one, even this car, is something that Clint felt we needed to go along with the requirements of his new position."

"It will be interesting to see what happens next," I said. "I'm anxious to get home. We'll take turns driving. If we're lucky, we'll be in Sabal late tomorrow."

Nell drove through familiar territory, and once we'd passed the D.C. metropolitan area, I took a turn driving while Nell rested. For the next sixteen hours or so, Nell and I existed in a bubble, wrapped inside Clint's car, stopping for bathroom breaks, gas, and food. We didn't talk much. We were comfortable enough with one another that we didn't need to.

When we finally pulled into Sabal, we were too tired to do much but greet Vaughn, Clint, and the kids. And then we both went to bed to get a solid sleep.

Later, when I awoke, I padded into the kitchen for a cup of coffee and heard Vaughn and Clint in the garage.

I followed their voices there and was pleased to see that Vaughn had cleared a section of the four-car air-conditioned garage for storing items from Nell and Clint's house.

"Hello," said Vaughn, walking over and wrapping his arms around me. "We've got the situation under control here. It'll be safe. I've hired a security team to keep a discreet eye on the house. No one will be breaking in here."

"Good," said Ann. "I must admit, it did feel uncomfortable being in a house that had been broken into. Nell doesn't know if she'll ever feel safe there."

"Thank you, Ann, for going with Nell to D.C. and helping her pack up a few of our belongings," said Clint. "I doubt anyone will try to break in again, but I like knowing the pieces she cares about are being protected here."

"How are you feeling?" I asked him, noting he was looking a little better.

"I'm not going to be doing any activities anytime soon, but the pain level is more manageable," he said. "I'm going to meet Claudine at the hotel tomorrow afternoon. In the meantime, Reggie and I have talked, and he agrees that there's been a substantial change to the agreement I made with the company for this project. He doesn't like it any better than I do."

"So, you'll meet with Claudine to go over that with her?" I asked.

"I want her to arrive at the same opinion as I have," Clint said. "But if she's playing a nasty game, as I suspect, it may lead to my resigning."

"Is that why the paperwork you wanted is so important?" I asked.

"Exactly," said Clint.

Nell joined us, and I left to go take a shower. Now that I'd had some rest, I was anxious to get to the hotel. We had a wedding in-house, and I was eager to see Rhonda and do my share of greeting guests.

I dressed for the wedding and drove to the hotel to meet Rhonda.

"How did it go in D.C.?" she asked when I walked into the office.

"Better than I expected. Nell is very organized, and we quickly packed up what she wanted to have here. As I told Vaughn, it made me uneasy to be in a house that had been broken into. Though it's a lovely home, Nell says she won't ever feel the same about it. But no matter what happens about any permanent move to Sabal, Nell now knows certain items she values are safe here."

"Will told me that Clint and Reggie met to go over Clint's work," Rhonda said. "I'm glad Clint is reaching out to him. Will and Reggie are known for their honesty."

"Yes, they are," I said. "Clint, too. That's why this situation is difficult for him. What's happening here at the hotel?"

"Claudine Everett is making her presence known by making demands. I understand that she and Clint are scheduled to meet here at the hotel tomorrow, and then I hope she'll move on. Otherwise, everything is going well. I met with Dorothy Stern. She and her friends are wrapping the gifts for the employees' Christmas party."

"How nice," I said. "She's a true treasure." Dorothy, a retired successful New York City businesswoman, volunteered to help us when we first opened by sending out brochures and doing other simple tasks. After she moved here, she told us she needed something to keep her busy. She'd worked for us ever since.

"We've got high tea to take care of tomorrow," I said. "Nell is scheduled to work on that."

"She has no problem doing that?" Rhonda asked.

"None. It might be a little chaotic and her long-range plans are on hold, but for now, she's happily settled here. It's not how she thought moving here would be, but it's exactly what she's wanted all along."

"Excellent. Because we need her," said Rhonda. "We have special luncheons and Christmas parties planned for every day for the next few weeks." She shook her head. "I easily forget how hectic these weeks are."

I grinned. "Maybe because it goes by in one big blur."

"When are Tina and her family coming?" asked Rhonda.

"I believe they'll arrive a couple of days before Christmas and leave right after New Year's Day," I said. "It'll be great to see them."

"I agree. They're like family," said Rhonda. She checked her watch. "We need to greet the wedding guests."

We tried to be present at weddings, greeting guests and ensuring everything ran smoothly. This kind of attention helped our business grow. And for Rhonda and me, it was a chance to show off the hotel we loved.

We walked into the lobby together and went to a group of people who were assembled there. Because it was a garden wedding, we'd lead them outdoors to be seated. Mingling among the guests, welcoming them to the hotel, and chatting with them about their stay, we made sure they were satisfied.

Just as we were about to lead the group outside, Claudine walked over to me.

"I see you're back from your trip. Can you tell me what's

going on?" she asked.

I blinked in surprise at her boldness and decided not to answer that question. "I understand you've been staying here. I hope everything is suitable. Clint tells us that he's meeting you here tomorrow."

"Yes. I didn't realize how bad his injuries were," said Claudine. "But we should be able to come to a quick agreement. After all, we've been working on this project for months."

"I'm sorry, but I must see to our guests," I said, trying to hide my distaste. I'd met plenty of egotistical people, but there was something really off about Claudine that I found unsettling.

"I think we should get to know one another," said Claudine. "And I'd like the opportunity to meet Vaughn."

"Annie, we have to go," said Rhonda, purposely interrupting us.

Seething beneath the surface at Claudine's behavior, I followed Rhonda outside to check on the wedding. Was Claudine so spoiled and entitled that she thought if she pushed and pushed, she'd get her way? Was that how she operated?

"I can't believe that woman," I said. "She's working to break up Nell's marriage and wants to meet her father. There's something very wrong with her."

"Ya got that right. I did you a real favor," said Rhonda. "If I'd stayed with Claudine another minute, I would've told her to eff off."

"I'd like to tell her myself. But now we have to be the sweet, caring hotel owners who want to make this wedding a very special occasion."

"The bride is lovely, and I like the groom," said Rhonda. "It's one of those sweet weddings. You'll see."

The ceremony was as touching as Rhonda had promised,

with the bride and groom obviously in love and not afraid to show it. I laughed with others in the crowd when the groom said, I do and swept his bride up into his arms and did a dizzying dance.

I thought back to Nell and Clint's wedding. The same kind of tender enthusiasm had been on display with them. Thank goodness they were working to make their relationship right again. But too often, couples couldn't get past that stage of needing different environments.

"Ready, Annie?" said Rhonda, elbowing me. "Let's get to the reception. Once it is running smoothly there, I'm going home."

"I'll help handle the bridal breakfast tomorrow, and then I'm taking the afternoon off."

Rhonda and I were careful about seeing that we each had periods away from the hotel. Being part of the day-in and day-out responsibilities could be exhausting. But owning and running the hotel filled a need in us that we recognized.

Until someone like Claudine entered the scene.

CHAPTER FIFTEEN

THE NEXT MORNING, I GOT UP EARLY AND SILENTLY MADE my way out of the house. It had been too long since I'd strolled the beach, and I needed to inhale the salty air and feel the sand between my toes in order to settle into my usual cheerful self.

I parked behind the hotel and waved to the security guard. Crossing the parking lot, I hurried to the sand, where I took off my sandals and set them aside.

Feeling the cool surface beneath my feet, I walked to the water's edge and stepped into its lacy pattern. The waves rolled onto shore, allowing water to play around my ankles. I was absorbed in watching the rhythmic movement when I felt someone's presence nearby and whipped around.

" 'Morning. What are you doing here?" I asked Claudine.

"I like to walk on the beach when only a few people are around," she said. "I met one of your neighbors earlier, and he mentioned you might be here."

"Are you talking about Brock Goodwin?" I asked her.

"Why, yes, that was his name. He said he was president of the Neighborhood Association and if I needed anything, I should talk to him."

I decided not to comment.

"Do you come here often?" Claudine asked me.

"Yes. It's a relaxing place to think."

Claudine kicked at the sand with a sneakered foot. "I know you don't like the thought of Clint and me being together, but we're good for one another."

"I think you're wrong about that. Nell and Clint are

happily married. Has he told you otherwise?" I asked.

"Not in so many words, but I can tell," Claudine said. "We work together very well and have a lot of fun doing it. He likes the same kind of lifestyle as I do. Together, we can make an impact in the business world."

"You'll have to excuse me. I need to get back to the hotel," I said abruptly. "I have commitments there."

"You'll see I'm right," said Claudine, giving me a steady look.

As I left her, my mind spun. Why in the world would this woman believe I would think she and Clint were good for one another if it meant breaking up his marriage? Had Clint said something to Claudine to make her believe that, or was the woman totally deranged and delusional?

I'd just finished seeing the last of the wedding guests escorted out of the library, where a breakfast buffet had been set up, when I saw Clint come into the hotel with Nell.

I walked over to greet them.

"You're here for your meeting with Claudine?" I asked Clint.

"Yes. We're meeting in one of the small conference rooms. I've resigned from the company, but felt it was only fair to tell Claudine in person," said Clint.

"I'll be working in the hospitality department," Nell told him, giving him a kiss. "Let me know when you're ready to go home."

After Nell left, I turned to Clint. "Claudine thinks you and she are going to be together. Why would she believe that unless you said something to her about it?"

Clint grimaced. "Believe me, I've never discussed a future together. She overheard an argument I had with Nell on the phone in my office. That's all. She has this insane desire to think of herself as irresistible when, in truth, she can be quite annoying. I'm not the first man in the company chased away by her weird behavior, claiming it was harassment. Now that the project we were working on has changed, I want no part of it. I emailed my resignation letter to HR and left messages for a few other people at the company."

"Thanks for clarifying. I'll show you to the conference rooms," I said, leading him from the lobby to a group of rooms at the end of a long hallway.

"Call me if you need anything," I said. "You have my number on your cell."

The door to the conference room was closed when we arrived. I opened the door for him and stepped back.

Claudine was sitting at the table inside wearing a low-cut sundress that showed off her cleavage. She patted the chair next to her. "Come sit down with me. I've been waiting for you. To celebrate, I've ordered coffee for us and a treat besides."

Clint remained standing. "I'm here to tell you in person that I've resigned from the company. I told you the other day that I wouldn't accept what the new numbers would mean for the people who worked at the company we were trying to buy."

"Business is business, Clint. You know that," chided Claudine. "You were brought on specifically for this project because of your contacts and your reputation for being fair. You must sign these papers. You're obligated to do so. Let me get you some coffee while you think about it."

She poured some coffee into a paper cup. "I'm serving it this way to make it easier for you to drink. Do you want me to help you?"

He shook his head and took a sip, then another. "I've already explained why I can't go along with these numbers. You've changed everything. Now, I can't honestly endorse it."

"What about us?" Claudine said.

"There is no us," said Clint. "There never was."

"But I overheard you tell Nell you couldn't live with her," said Claudine.

"That was in the heat of anger, and we've resolved the issues that were coming between us," said Clint. "Besides, it was a conversation you should never have overheard. It was supposed to be in the privacy of my office."

I stood frozen in place. When Claudine started to cry, I eased away from the doorway. This, too, was a private conversation.

When I walked back into my office, I was surprised to see Rhonda. " 'Morning. I didn't expect to see you here. I thought you were going to try to take the day off."

"I've been thinking about Clint," said Rhonda. "Will told me Clint's resigning from his job and the project he was working on. I've had some worrying thoughts. Nothing specific, but I want to be here."

I felt my heart stop and then start up again. Rhonda's intuitions were usually spot on.

"The wedding party that just left was a very easy one," said Rhonda. "Too bad all of them couldn't be like that. I want to be sure the hospitality department writes them a thank you note."

"Yes. It's important to follow up with other members of the wedding party, as well. You never know when we'll get another wedding out of that group."

My cell rang. *Clint.*

"Hi, what's up?" I asked.

"Help me," Clint said in a soft voice and then went silent.

I gaped at Rhonda and waved her out of her chair. "C'mon. Clint needs help."

We trotted down to the conference room and looked inside.

Clint's face was turned away from us, his upper body sprawled on the conference table.

"Clint! What happened?" I said, rushing to him.

"I think I've been drugged. I can't move. Help me. I'm going to be sick."

Rhonda and I got him to his feet and to the bathroom in the hallway outside the door.

A few minutes later, Clint emerged from the bathroom looking ghostly white. "Claudine must've slipped something in my coffee. She made me sign the new contract. I need to get to her to retrieve those papers. She's probably on her way to Miami."

"Rhonda, you stay with Clint. I'm going to see if she's checked out," I said, and sprinted away.

I hurried to the front desk. "Has Claudine Everett checked out?

"Yes, a few minutes ago," said one of the clerks. "She left in her fancy car."

"Thanks," I said, and trotted back to Rhonda and Clint.

"She left moments ago in her car," I said. "We might be able to catch her."

"You drive," said Rhonda, putting an arm around Clint's waist and leading him to the back of the hotel.

"Should I tell Nell?" I asked Clint.

"Not yet," said Clint. "We need to catch Claudine. I need those papers back. I'll never be able to work for anyone else again if I get caught up in that bad deal."

As soon as Clint settled in the backseat of my car and Rhonda had buckled herself into the passenger seat, I took off.

"Chances are she's using Alligator Alley," said Rhonda. "If so, we should be able to catch her. I'm going to make a call to remind the State Troopers."

I drove through town, and once we reached the point where Alligator Alley began, and I had a clear view of the road ahead, I accelerated.

"I'm sorry for this," said Clint. "I can hardly believe the situation I'm in. I should never have taken this job and invested in the project. And now I just want to get out of it."

"If something seems too good to be true, there's usually a reason behind it. Not always a wise choice," Rhonda said. "But you've resigned. Right?"

"The board wants me to make an appearance before they officially release me. I told them I'd come to D.C. as soon as the doctor gives me permission to travel." He lifted his right arm in his soft cast. "This isn't the problem. My other arm is."

I glanced at Clint in the backseat through the rearview mirror. Stress and pain had taken a toll on him. He looked older and more vulnerable than I'd ever seen him.

"You and Nell and the kids can stay at the house as long as you need to," I said.

"Thanks. Nell and I talked most of last night," said Clint. "With my financial background, I've already spoken to Reggie and Will about working with them. It won't be the glamorous job I'm leaving, but it's an honest one with room for growth."

"What kind of car does Claudine have?" I asked Clint.

"She drives a sporty silver BMW." He peered ahead. "I think that's her ahead of us in the distance."

I pressed down on the accelerator. Claudine had no problem playing dirty. When called upon, Rhonda and I could step up our game.

I passed Claudine and then slowed down, making her slow as well and forcing her to the side of the road, where I stopped my car.

Rhonda got out and walked over to the driver's side of Claudine's vehicle.

When Claudine noticed her, she gunned her engine and prepared to back up her car to get away, just as a Florida Highway Patrol car pulled up behind her.

Rhonda waved to the State Trooper. "Hi, John. Thanks for coming. We have a problem here."

"What's going on, Rhonda?" he asked. Tall, with broad shoulders and thick gray hair, he took off his sunglasses and smiled at her.

"Miss Everett has some paperwork we need," said Rhonda. "She obtained a signature under duress."

The officer walked over to Claudine's car. "Please get out of the car, ma'am. We need to talk to you."

As Claudine stepped out onto the verge, I helped Clint out of the car, and we joined them.

Claudine whipped around and faced him with a scowl. "You! What do you have to do with this?"

"You know damn well what you did in order to get my signature on those papers," Clint said.

Claudine turned to the trooper. "Officer, do I look like the kind of woman who would do something bad?"

The trooper gave her a steady look. "I learned a long time ago not to judge someone by their appearance."

Clint stepped forward. "I was in a meeting with this woman not long ago. She served us coffee, and shortly afterwards, I felt a strange sensation, as if I were suspended in time. Something like that. She pushed papers in front of me and forced me to sign them."

"And then what happened?" the officer asked.

"She left, and a few minutes later, I called Ann Sanders for help," said Clint. "I felt too sick to run after Claudine."

"When Clint told me what had happened, it made sense to me because I was aware of an earlier conversation between them. Ms. Everett has been under the wrong impression about their relationship and refuses to believe his sincerity about being unwilling to sign the revised business documents."

Rhonda said, "John, you know Annie and I have no reason to lie to you."

He turned to Claudine. "What do you have to say for yourself?"

Claudine broke down, covering her face with her hands as she sobbed. "I need to be successful with this project, or I will be forced out of the company. My father never wanted me to be part of it. He's unhappy with the projects I've worked on. He thinks I should get married, stay away from the business, and give him grandchildren."

Tears streamed down Claudine's cheeks. She glanced around at us. "Nothing I do is ever good enough. I hate being compared to my perfect, dead sister. The one he always loved more than me. I'm so tired of being a failure."

The trooper looked uncomfortable. "Rhonda, do you or this gentleman want to press charges?"

We all turned to face Clint.

He shook his head. "I just need those signed papers returned to me so I can destroy them. I want as little to do with Claudine Everett and her father's business as possible."

The trooper studied Claudine. "Is that fine with you?"

Still visibly shaken, she sniffled, nodded, and hung her head.

We stood by as she reached inside her car for her briefcase and opened it, placing it on the hood of the car.

Carefully, Clint and I went through the paperwork and removed the documents he wanted.

"Okay," said the trooper. "That's settled then. Are we all in agreement?"

We indicated so, and then Rhonda, Clint, and I returned to my car.

"How am I ever going to thank the two of you?" Clint asked as I helped buckle him in the backseat. "I've totally screwed up."

"Listen, kiddo," said Rhonda. "It's one of those fucking life lessons. Learn from it."

"You have a chance to make the changes you and Nell both want,," I said. "Make that fresh start work for you."

Clint nodded. "I'm not sure how it's all going to evolve, but I want to make it right."

We were quiet as we headed back. Nothing more really needed to be said.

At home, Clint went to his room to lie down, and Vaughn and I watched Bailey and Ned in the pool, while Robbie was with his friend next door. Having a swimming pool meant making sure visiting children could swim. Both of Nell's children had learned at an early age. And though they were capable swimmers, we always made sure to watch them.

When Nell called to tell me that she was on her way home, I told her about our plans to take Robbie, Bailey, and Ned to Robbie's favorite pizza restaurant and then to the movies.

"Thanks. Clint spoke to me earlier, but as you said, we need to talk privately." Nell cleared her throat. "I knew it was a bad idea for him to work for the company. Now, we'll really have to listen to one another."

That night, as I lay in bed beside Vaughn, he turned to me. "Thanks for being such a big support to Nell. It means a lot to me to know that she has your help navigating through this challenge. Nell is a lot like Ellie was—easygoing to a certain point, then watch out."

"Clint knows he's really screwed up and wants to make Nell happy. That will go a long way with her. Like we agreed earlier, we have to let them work it out. And if they end up with a much simpler lifestyle, that's how it'll be. Agreed?"

"Yes," said Vaughn. "That's how this whole debacle started, with Clint feeling he couldn't support Nell as she wanted."

"A completely false assumption," I said. "The weeks ahead are going to be busy. Let's enjoy them."

"Okay. I'm going to start doing that right away. Come here," said Vaughn, drawing me closer to him.

CHAPTER SIXTEEN

THE STAFF CHRISTMAS PARTY WAS A FAVORITE EVENT FOR our employees and for Rhonda and me. Even Vaughn played a part, dressing up like Santa Claus to hand out gifts to all their children.

This year was even more exciting for me because Bailey and Ned were living with us, and that made the magic of the season even more real.

When I checked in with Annette at the hotel to see how the plans were shaping up, she said, "Very well. In fact, we have a surprise for you and Rhonda."

"It's a secret?" I asked.

"Definitely," she answered, wearing an enigmatic smile.

I, who hadn't had childlike holidays growing up with my stern grandmother, grinned back. "I can't wait to see it."

"It'll be worth the wait," said Annette, laughing.

Later, when I told Rhonda about it, she said, "Guess that's why it's a surprise. No one will give me a hint about it. Clearly, we'll have to wait a couple more days to find out."

On the late afternoon of the day of the party, we closed the dining room. We were going to transform it into a holiday scene with presents placed around the Christmas tree that stood in the corner of the main room. Buffet tables were lined against the wall, and a special cookie table was set up in a corner for the children. A bar serving beer, wine, and punch was located near a table offering coffee, tea, and cocoa. If anyone overindulged in alcohol, we had drivers ready to deliver them home, but with it being a family affair, we seldom had that kind of trouble.

As usual, Rhonda and I arranged to arrive early to greet our employees' families together. Today, she was wearing a crimson caftan while I'd slipped on a dark green sheath in keeping with holiday colors.

"You look festive," I said, giving her a hug. "I never grow tired of doing this party for our employees."

"Same," said Rhonda. "The kids look forward to it as much or more than their parents."

"And we all have a fun time," I said, watching the young, single wait staff put out the food. We'd learned long ago to feed the crowd first, then open the gifts.

Families were lined up outside the doors when Rhonda and I finally opened them to welcome the people inside.

Noticing children in new dressy clothes, a sweetness filled me. They looked excited to be here. Though some of them tried not to show it, most of the teenagers in the group seemed pleased to be among the group of kids and parents.

Angie and Liz arrived with their children, followed by Nell, Clint, and the kids, accompanied by Vaughn and Robbie.

Once the room was full, Bernie went to the microphone and welcomed everyone to the party. It seemed only right for him to speak as he was the leader of our employees.

Later, as people were continuing to eat the ham, turkey, and beef that had been served, Rhonda went to the microphone.

"Happy holidays to everyone! Annie and I always look forward to this party because ... presents for the kids!"

The kids erupted into cheers. Adults looked on as Rhonda explained how, when a child's name was called, they'd move forward, receive their gift, and bring it back to their parents to open it, keeping the process going.

I went into the back hall to greet Vaughn, dressed as Santa. He looked adorable in the suit that did a decent job of covering him up.

"We'll have you sit right by the tree," I said, looking with surprise at the big elf following Vaughn into the room.

Laughter bubbled out of me as I stared at Bernie dressed in a green and white striped costume and wearing big red booties on his feet.

Rhonda came over to us. "Bernie! You're the surprise!"

Bernie nodded sheepishly. "I got talked into doing this by the staff."

I clapped my hands together. "It's perfect. You're a doll to go along with it."

Bernie shook his head. "I would only do this for the two of you. It's been a helluva ride."

The kids gathered around the tree, sitting on the floor or standing nearby as Vaughn called out one name after another. With a total of over seventy children, it was smart that Bernie was able to smooth the operation by handing a gift to the appropriate child. There were even a few bicycles and tricycles involved.

When it was the Ts's turn to receive their gifts, I helped ensure they got the right ones and led them back to Liz and Chad. Their little brother, Gabe, was given his gift in his mother's arms.

Nell helped Bailey and Ned with their gifts, and then the last one was given to Robbie.

"Last but not least," I said, giving him a hug.

I stood a moment and watched Bernie help a child open his package. Unexpected tears stung my eyes. Bernie was such a wonderful man, who'd changed a lot from when we first met him. Gone was the stiff, proper man who lived by strict rules. In his place was a softer, gentler man who Rhonda and I treasured.

Rhonda sidled up to me and stood watching Bernie. "What a great surprise to see him dressed in costume like this. It's made this Christmas special already."

"It was a lucky day when we hired him to be our general manager," I said.

"I hope he and Annette like the cruise we're giving them," said Rhonda. "It's the least we can do."

"They'll love it," I said. "Now, let's get the families moving out of here so we can put the dining room in order."

Rhonda and I stood by the doors wishing people goodnight. I couldn't help thinking how fortunate we were to have loyal staff members. Most of them had been with us for years; some, from the beginning.

When I arrived home, the family was gathered on the lanai watching a holiday special. I walked over to the couch and sat down beside Vaughn. This, being here together, was the best gift of all.

The next day, Nell and Clint flew to D.C., leaving Bailey and Ned in our care.

Clint was now wearing removable casts on both arms and had begun very light physical therapy to keep his shoulder joints flexible. He was anxious to meet with the board of his company and sever that relationship completely.

Nell was meeting with the real estate agent to sign the appropriate paperwork for the sale of the house. A family from outside the country was interested in buying it for a fair price, along with a lot of Nell and Clint's furniture. Nell was hoping to close the deal so she could begin looking for a house in Sabal. With a second mortgage placed on the house in D.C., her hopes for finding what she thought she wanted were slim.

That evening, Nell called me. "We're here, staying at the house. It seems strange to be in it, knowing we'll soon be gone.

Sitting beside Clint on the plane, I thought of the past year and all we'd been through, and I've never felt closer to him."

"It's important for the two of you to have some time alone," I told her. "Don't worry about the kids. They're busy with us, Liana, and our special grandparents, who are loving being with them."

After we ended the call, I told Vaughn that having Nell and Clint work together to move on with their lives was very hopeful.

"Now, we must let them handle their circumstances."

I chuckled. "I know, I know. But parents want their children to be content and settled."

He wrapped his arms around me. "You're such a good mom." I leaned against him, thinking how incredible it was to have found him and his two children.

Liz called as I was tucking Bailey and Ned into bed. It being a school night, they were more than ready to go to sleep. Meeting new kids at school was exciting for them, but also nerve-racking. Especially for Bailey, who was used to her friends at home. Ned's first-grade teacher was a favorite, and I didn't worry about him finding friends.

I kissed them goodnight and took the call from Liz. "Hi, what's up?"

"I just learned that elderly people in my neighborhood are going to sell their house and move to a 55+ community nearby. I know Nell is looking for a house, and though this house is a real 'fixer-upper', I want her to know about it. I've tried her cell and no answer."

"Keep trying. I love your neighborhood," I said, vowing not to get any more involved than necessary. I'd promised Vaughn.

The next morning, I was surprised by an early call from Nell, who informed me that the house was going up for sale in

Liz's neighborhood. "Would you go take a look at it for Clint and me? We trust your judgment."

"Sure. I'll call Liz and make those arrangements. Then, I'll let you know what I think. Hopefully, they'll let me take some photos, too."

"Thanks, Ann. I knew I could count on you. Clint and I will sign the sales agreement for this house today. Once that's done, I'll know how much we'll have to spend on a new one."

I ended the call with Nell and phoned Liz.

"I've already spoken to the owners and told them I have someone interested in buying their house and that we might not need a realtor, only a lawyer, which would be cheaper. They're very excited."

"Let me know what time to come and see the house for Nell and Clint. I've got a meeting with some magazine people, but no matter when you arrange a visit, I'll be there. This is too important."

"I hope they'll be willing to work on the house," said Liz. "It's the best location for a family. Everyone in the neighborhood is extremely friendly. They'll fit right in."

"We can only do so much, but I appreciate your quick thinking. What Nell and Clint decide will be up to them."

"Oops, gotta go. I'll call you in a bit," said Liz, and I heard a chorus of cries in the background.

Rhonda and I were meeting with the advertising people from one of the society magazines we advertised in when Liz rang my cell to tell me to come to the house right now.

I stood. "May Rhonda and I get back to you with our decision on what and when we'll advertise? I have another meeting I can't miss."

The magazine's salespeople quickly agreed, and after walking them out of the office, I turned to Rhonda. "Want to come with me to take a peek at the house Liz has in mind for Nell and Clint?"

"Do I ever," said Rhonda. "Angie called me this morning to tell me about it."

"Great." No matter what was happening at the hotel, our children came first.

A few minutes later, I drove into the neighborhood where both Liz and Angela lived with their families. It was attractive and clearly a place for young people. Tricycles and bicycles were in front of many of the houses, along with a few strollers.

Liz was already at the house when I pulled up in front of a smaller home that needed fresh paint. It had an outdated front patio on which two rocking chairs sat.

I turned to Rhonda. "Liz called it a 'fixer upper'. I can see why."

Liz met us by the sidewalk leading up to the front door. "It was built the same year as my house, and I'm sure it must have a sound structure. The builder is well known for that. The owners are a very nice couple, but they haven't been able to upgrade or maintain the house."

After Liz rang the doorbell, a sweet-faced older woman answered the door. Her blue-eyed gaze swept the three of us.

"Ah, Elizabeth. And this must be your mother and her friend, Rhonda. I'm Hester Wiley. Come in. Don't mind, Earl. He's napping in his chair. As you can see, this house should go to a young, energetic couple as Liz described."

Ann gazed around the living room, trying to ignore the magazines, the knitting, and the books everywhere. The layout of the entrance, living room, and beyond to the kitchen and dining area had a nice flow to it. One side of the front entry hall had a small powder room tucked beneath the stairs that led to a second story.

"The master suite is on the first floor. Upstairs, there are three bedrooms and two baths," Hester explained. "We kept that floor for family visits. Earl and I haven't been up there in a long time, but feel free to take a look. If we can sell this house directly without having people troop through at all times, we'd be glad to do it."

"What are you asking?" I asked her.

"Our son says to stand firm on $325,000, no matter what," said Hester.

I knew Nell and Clint's house in Maryland cost a lot more than that, but I didn't know the amount of their second mortgage.

"Let's take a look at the second floor," said Liz.

Rhonda, Liz, and I climbed the stairs to what looked like a scene from the past. It was obvious that Hester and Earl had two girls and one boy. Their rooms hadn't changed much at all. Two of the rooms had walls painted pink or purple. In the pink room, posters of various actors and rock stars from years ago covered some of the paint. In the purple room, there were still horse statues sitting on top of the bureau.

We moved to the boy's room, painted blue with posters of baseball players Alex Rodriguez, Josh Hamilton, and Derrick Rose. A baseball trophy sat on the top of a chest of drawers painted white.

I found it both touching and disturbing that the rooms had been kept like that and wondered how often Earl and Hester's children actually visited. Each of the bedrooms would need to be painted and either have new carpeting or flooring installed. The smallest bedroom would make a great office.

The two bathrooms would need to be upgraded, though both were functional.

Rhonda didn't speak, but I could tell from her expression that she was as surprised as I to find the house in such condition.

Downstairs, we inspected the kitchen, laundry room, and

master suite. These were in much better condition and had been recently upgraded, which made me feel better.

The two-car garage was surprisingly empty except for the Prius parked there.

"The backyard is big enough for a pool," Hester explained. "We were thinking of putting one in when Earl was laid off from work on disability, and we couldn't do it."

That explained a lot about the lack of upgrades.

"Thank you for letting us see the house. My daughter will be in touch with us, and we'll provide you with an answer within twenty-four hours. Will that do?"

"Oh, yes," said Hester. "You know what we want for the house."

"Yes. You made that clear," I said.

Liz said, "I have a lawyer lined up in case this sale works for both you and my sister."

"Thank you," said Hester, leading us to the front door. Earl remained in his chair asleep. Outside, Rhonda, Liz, and I met by my car and stood talking about the house.

"A home inspector will be able to identify any problems that need to be addressed," said Rhonda. "But though the house needs to be painted and spruced up inside, it seems to be well-built."

"For that amount of money, the house is a steal. But Nell and Clint will have to put quite a bit of money into the house to bring it up to the standards of the neighborhood," said Liz. "But if they're willing to work on it, the house is an excellent buy."

"I think so, too," I said to her. "Clint is the one you have to convince. He wanted a bigger house than they already had in a better neighborhood when they moved a couple of years ago. And though this house is very different from what they have, it can be stunning."

"I don't think we should send any photos to Nell now,"

said Rhonda. "See if the numbers work for them, and then send her the photos we took along with a list of what renovations we think they'll need to make."

"Okay," I said. Looking back at the house, I saw how beautiful it could be.

"Okay, I'm going to call Nell," said Liz. "I told her I would."

"We'd better get back to the hotel," said Rhonda. "We have a big luncheon going on, and we need to make our presence known."

Alone in the car, I said, "Once I got past what the interior looked like, I fell in love with the house. I can picture Nell living there, where the children can easily find friends to play with."

"Me, too," said Rhonda. "But it will be a big change for Clint. Do you think he'll do it?"

CHAPTER SEVENTEEN

THAT EVENING, VAUGHN AND I SAT ON THE COUCH ON THE lanai and discussed the Wiley's house. I showed him a couple of photos that I'd taken and explained that Earl had been laid off on disability some years ago, and he and Hester had done very little upgrading on the first floor and almost none on the second floor.

"But the layout and bones of the house are excellent. The backyard can accommodate a pool, and I noticed plenty of storage space," I said enthusiastically.

"You've done what Nell asked of you," said Vaughn. "Now, we have to let them make their own decision about it."

"Agreed. Because if they decide to go ahead with the purchase, it'll take a lot of work on their part to get it the way they are sure to want it. And right now, Clint can do very little until he's healed, leaving most of the work to Nell."

"I still feel bad about those injuries," admitted Vaughn.

I patted his arm. "It was just a freaky accident."

Bailey and Ned ran into the room in their pajamas and climbed up on the couch with us. "Ready for bed?" I asked. They'd been allowed to watch a television show with Robbie.

I walked them to their bathroom and watched as they brushed their teeth. It was such a treat having them with us. Without their parents around, they were especially eager to cuddle and talk about their lives at home. The move to Florida would be healthy for both Bailey and her brother, because they'd been well aware of the tension inside their home.

"Gammy, will you read to us?" asked Ned.

"Of course. One short book because you have school tomorrow," I said.

"I have a new friend," said Ned. "His name is Jacob."

"I have two new friends," Bailey said. "But I'll make more. The girls here are cool. Not like some of the girls back home."

Interesting, I thought. "It's very sweet when you make new friends. Girls and boys are the same everywhere. They want to be liked and treated with kindness."

"That's what my teacher, Miss Ortiz, says," Bailey announced.

"Let's pick a book to read," I said.

"How about this one?" said Ned, holding up *Stellaluna*.

"Perfect," I said, climbing onto the bed with a child on each side of me. It was moments like this when I realized how lucky I was. My grandmother would read to me as a child, but we never cuddled in bed like this.

I'd just turned out the lights in their rooms when my cell rang with Nell's specific chime.

"Hello," I said. "Is everything all right?"

"It's both good and bad," Nell said. "We signed the sales agreement for the house with a closing date of January 15th. I've hired a moving company to help us after the first of the year."

"But?" I asked.

"But Clint's company is threatening to sue him for breach of contract. Clint's lawyer friend agrees it would never hold up in court, but they're using it to stall returning his share of equity contribution. Again, Clint's lawyer doesn't think they can legally do that. But it means we can't use that money for a new house."

"Mrs. Wiley told me she's going to stand firm on her price. Can you meet that number?" I asked her.

"Yes, but we'll have very little money for renovations right away," said Nell.

"The house is in fine shape overall. It just needs a lot of decorating with painted walls, flooring, and the like."

"That's the problem. Clint can't do any of the work right now. And he likes everything to be nice," said Nell.

"Because something is in a state of transition doesn't mean it can't be," I said.

"I know," said Nell. "I'm working on the numbers now. We know from Liz that the house is a great buy even in its present condition. If a home inspection doesn't turn up anything major, it's a find. I love her neighborhood and the idea of the children being together."

"Let me know what you and Clint decide," I said. After I ended the call, I decided to say as little as possible about the situation to anyone else. I wanted to give Nell and Clint the opportunity to work it out for themselves.

The next morning, I felt as if I needed to take a walk on the beach before going into work. The morning temperatures in December were cool enough to wear a sweater or jacket, and after dressing, I slipped on my favorite jean jacket and headed out.

As I stepped onto the beach, I saw only a few people jogging along the sand, and I let out a sigh of satisfaction. I'd spent a restless night thinking of Nell and hoping they'd decide to buy the Wiley's house. It would be a change for them to a simpler, less glamorous lifestyle, but I knew it would be a wise move for all of them.

Feeling the cool sea breezes against my cheeks as I jogged along the edge of the water deep in thought, I was startled to hear my name called from right behind me. *Nooo!*

I whipped around and faced Brock Goodwin.

"'Morning, Ann, I was hoping to see you here. You missed out on buying my fireworks, but my import company is offering some Valentine's decorations. I know you have a big party each year, and I'd like to meet with you and Rhonda to show you some attractive items."

I studied him, trying to control my temper. How dare he pretend he hadn't recently tried to harm our hotel by collaborating with the chef of an Italian restaurant to undermine us? "Thanks, but no thanks. As you must know, we have our party supplier."

Brock frowned and shook a finger at me. "Look, I know we haven't always been the best of friends, but I'd like to start all over again with you and Rhonda. You can be good for my business, and my business can benefit you."

"Like I said, Brock, thanks, but no thanks. See you later."

He shook his head. "You'll be sorry. Just saying."

I headed back to the hotel in an easy jog, though I wanted to sprint as fast as possible. There was something so dishonest about the man that I felt goosebumps crawl over my skin even as I warmed up from my run.

Later, when I walked into the office, Rhonda was on the phone. I could tell from the flush on her cheeks that she was upset. "No, Brock, we aren't interested. I've got to go. Someone just walked into my office," said Rhonda, ending the call with a grimace.

"Did he want to sell you Valentine supplies?" I asked, taking a seat behind my desk.

"Yes. He said he missed seeing you at the beach and wanted to speak to me," said Rhonda.

"What a liar. I saw him on the beach earlier this morning and told him we weren't interested." I let out a long sigh. "Why doesn't he understand that he can't treat people badly and then expect them to support his business?"

"He never will," said Rhonda. "Any news about Nell and the house?"

"I talked to her last night, and she promised to tell me when they've made a decision," I said.

"Angie says it's a terrific buy at that price. I hope they decide to go for it," said Rhonda. "And I know you've wanted them to move to Sabal for a long time."

"It would be a dream come true," I said, and changed the subject. "Our cancer awareness lunch is today. Are you planning to attend?"

"Yes. It's a group dear to my heart after I had that awful scare," said Rhonda. "I understand Vaughn has agreed to attend as their guest speaker."

"Yes," I said. "He does a few fundraisers each year, and because of Ellie, cancer awareness is important to him."

"I spoke to Lorraine this morning. She's going to be working part-time for the next few weeks, even though we suggested she wait to come back to work after Arthur's death."

"That will actually be helpful because, as it looks right now, Nell will be busy with the move from their house in D.C. to here. They've signed the sales agreement."

"That's a big step in the right direction," said Rhonda. She held up a sheaf of papers. "Let's review the figures for high tea. We might need to reduce the number of staff for them."

We were working on the financial projections for the tea events when Liz called. "Clint has agreed to buy the Wiley's house!" Excitement rang in her voice. "Oh, Mom, I'm thrilled. I've wanted Nell to move to Sabal for forever."

"That's wonderful news," I said. "Are they working with your lawyer?"

"Yes. It's a tricky situation because they can't buy the Wiley house until January when Hester and Earl are ready to move and their own house in D.C. is ready to sell."

"That makes sense. Have you told Vaughn yet?" I asked Liz.

"No, but I'm going to call him next. See you later," Liz

said, ending the call.

I sat back in my chair and let out a sigh of relief. It was still only an idea, but one that could be rewarding for my family.

At lunchtime, Rhonda and I joined the other attendees, mostly female, for the Cancer Awareness luncheon. I sat with Vaughn at one of the tables for eight. Seeing how the other women at the table fussed over him, I was struck by the realization that to them, he was a movie star, while to me, he was just Vaughn, the man I lived with, slept with, and loved. I'd long since given up being jealous when women flirted with him. It came with the job. At home with his family, there was no doubt about his loyalty to them and to me.

After lunch, as I watched Vaughn speak about the importance of supporting cancer research and how his first wife, Ellie, had died from cancer, I loved how he glanced at me. I owed a lot to Ellie for teaching Vaughn humility at home while being adored in public. I would always think of her fondly.

I gazed around the room, noting who, in the community, was there. Rhonda and I encouraged luncheons like this, and I was pleased to see many people I knew. I'd come to Sabal not knowing anyone but Rhonda and Angie. Now, my life seemed full of friends.

After the meal, Dorothy Stern came over to me. "It's a generous group this year. Thanks to the support you and Rhonda give to it." She held up the small gold silk bag that we'd provided for each guest. The bag contained coupons and small gifts from businesses throughout the community, and a small bottle of expensive perfume from us. Brock had wanted us to include a plastic toy from his import business, but Dorothy had turned him down.

While Vaughn was busy talking to people, I left the room to see how our dinner for the evening was shaping up. A group of lawyers had booked the private dining room for a year-end holiday event. Between the high-end meal they ordered and the alcohol they would consume, it was a very profitable deal for us.

Rhonda followed me into the small dining room, my favorite room in the hotel. Decorated for the holidays, greens, gold ribbons, and glass balls filled the room with holiday spirit, accentuating the pale gold color of the walls and the rich walnut wood of the dining room furniture.

"I've got to leave," said Rhonda. "Sally Kate has a classroom play I promised to attend."

"I'm elated she's doing well at her new school," I said. Sally Kate struggled with dyslexia, and Angie and Rhonda had found the perfect teacher for her at a private school in town.

Rhonda and I parted ways, and I decided to go see Liz to talk about the house Nell and Clint wanted to buy. It was hard being this close to having a dream of mine come true, knowing obstacles still lay ahead.

CHAPTER EIGHTEEN

When I walked into Liz's house, I was met by the excited cries of my grandchildren.

"Gammy, I want this book," said Gabe, toddling to me holding a picture book for me to read.

"Will you play Candyland with us?" asked Emma.

Laughing, I hugged each child. "Let me talk to your mother first. Then I'll read and play with you." Having these grandchildren close by meant the world to me. And thinking of Bailey and Ned living in Sabal was another part of the dream.

Liz found us in the playroom. "Hi, Mom! I'm glad you're here. I was just on the phone with Hester Wiley, and she has agreed for me to come and measure the rooms and make some notes on the conditions for Nell. Chad is working at home today and can watch the kids. Will you join me?"

"Sure," I said. "So, everyone has agreed to proceed with the sale?"

"Yes. Our lawyer is drafting a sales agreement with all the standard contingencies. A home inspection has been scheduled, and Nell and Clint have already approved paying a deposit large enough to help the Wileys with their move."

"Okay. Let me say goodbye to the children, and I'll go with you," I said. "I'm going to run an errand with your mother," I told them. "When I return, I'll play with you."

"Promise?" said Olivia.

"I promise all of you," I said, eager to give my attention to them.

###

Liz drove me to the Wiley's house, and we sat a moment while Liz went over a list of instructions she'd put together.

"In addition to the size of the rooms, Nell wants us to check for the condition of the wooden trim, floors, or carpeting, and light fixtures," Liz said. "She wants to be as realistic as possible when talking about the cost of upgrades because she can't do everything at once."

"The home inspector will check over the appliances," I said. "I noticed the house needs painting, but the roof and the condition of the exterior walls looked fine."

"The home inspector will double-check that," said Liz. "Should we be looking at anything else?"

I mentally retraced my steps from when I'd visited earlier. "The upstairs bathrooms need dressing up, though that's something that might have to wait. I want to take a closer look at the landscaping. We might be able to get Manny and his crew to lend some help there."

"The kitchen is only a few years old," said Liz. "The appliances are fairly new. The washing machine and dryer are not."

"Okay, I'm set to go. I'll tell you when I want you to write something down," I said.

We got out of the car and headed to the front door.

A kind-faced older gentleman greeted us. "This must be Liz and ..."

"I'm her mother, Ann Sanders," I said, extending my hand. "And you are Earl."

Chuckling, he shook my hand. "Guess I was napping when you came earlier."

"We didn't want to disturb you," Liz said. "We hope we're not disturbing you now."

"No, no. Not at all. Come in and do what you need to do." He held the door open, and when we went inside, I noticed how tidy the living room was.

"We're pretty excited about being able to sell the house this way," said Earl. "Let me know if you need anything. Hester has gone to the grocery store, but she'll be right back."

"Let's start in the kitchen," I said to Liz.

There, we measured the dining space and checked the appliances, cupboards, and drawers. It was in acceptable condition with more than adequate storage for a family. It would be a huge relief for Nell.

As we went through the house, my initial impressions were right. It would take work and creativity, but beneath its faded, outdated appearance was a very nice home.

When we were through with the interior, we thanked Earl and Hester and walked around the outside. Some of the overgrown landscaping would need to be removed, but I'd already thought of giving Nell and Clint a housewarming gift of having Manny work on their yard.

We sat in the car outside Liz's house, comparing notes and ideas to share with Nell.

"Furniture is something else Nell is going to have to deal with," said Liz. "The family buying their house wanted all the furniture in the dining room, living room, and guest rooms, and whatever else Nell and Clint are willing to sell."

"I'm satisfied that we've done what we could to help with her decisions," I told Liz. "But if you need anything else from me, you know how eager I am to help. Having you two sisters living close together is thrilling for me. Right now, I'm going inside to see my adorable grandchildren."

Liz laughed. "You wouldn't think they were adorable if you had to wake them up for school."

"You were a sleepyhead, too," I said, patting her back. In truth, she was an easy child, as if to make up for the loss of other babies.

Inside, I went to the playroom and made myself

comfortable on the soft carpet. The Ts got out the Candyland game, and with Gabe on my lap, I settled down to play with them.

As I drove home, I hoped Bailey and Ned would agree to play a different game from Candyland tonight. Still, knowing they were at the house to greet me filled me with joy.

I'd just pulled into my driveway when Rhonda called me. "Hi, Annie. You'll never guess what's happened. I got a call from a friend at the Chamber of Commerce who wanted me to know they received an email complaining about service at The Beach House Hotel."

"Really? From whom?" I asked.

"Claudine Everett. She claimed she was treated poorly, that you and I personally interfered with a business deal signed at the hotel. Can you believe that?" said Rhonda. "What a bitch."

"She has a lot of nerve," I said. "I guess she's fighting for her job, striking out at anyone she can. One thing is for certain. We have proof of what actually happened, courtesy of a state trooper and the body camera footage. There's no disputing that."

"Yeah, I hadn't thought of that. Still, it burns my butt that she's trying to harass us," said Rhonda.

"As Bernie would say, we'll simply carry on," I said, but I was as mad as Rhonda. We ran our hotel impeccably and took pride in doing so. We didn't need Claudine making twisted accusations about us or The Beach House Hotel. "Our best response is no response."

"Right. I told Will about it, and he said the same thing." Rhonda let out a long breath. "You should've seen Sally Kate in the school play. She was adorable and had memorized her two lines perfectly."

"Excellent," I said. "When I see her, I'll be sure to

congratulate her, if I get a chance while all the kids are playing together."

Rhonda laughed. "Thanks. She'll love that anytime."

Rhonda and I ended our call, and I tried to put myself in a lighter mood before going in and facing my family. But I knew Claudine's action wasn't the only one Rhonda and I might have to deal with regarding Everett, Shuster, and Donnelly. Aware of how they were treating Clint, I was beginning to understand what kind of company it was.

Later, Nell phoned the children to say goodnight and then asked to speak to me.

"Hi, Ann. I want to thank you for helping Liz take measurements and make notes for our new house. It'll help me a lot to plan what we need to do for the move."

"When are you coming back to Sabal?" I asked her.

"I'm going to fly out tomorrow afternoon. Clint will have to stay here in D.C. to meet with his lawyer. He says he'll be fine, but he's still finding it awkward to do simple tasks. He wants me to send him copies of the agreements with the company, but wants to retain the originals in case this issue goes to court."

"Oh, but I thought it would be a simple matter of resigning," I said, alarmed.

"They're going to fight it, telling him he can't resign until the project is complete and saying that he can't get back his equity investment in the company. It's a disaster," said Nell.

"How's Clint handling it?" I asked.

"Not well. He's furious with them and himself," said Nell. "I told him the best revenge is to move forward. That's why I'm pushing to get that house, even though I know in its present condition, it's not what we hoped for."

"It's going to be a lovely home," I said.

"I know it, but Clint sees it as another of his mistakes in leaving his old job to take a chance on this newer one. I'm trying to convince him otherwise, but in truth, we wouldn't be in this trouble if he'd listened to me. But I can't say that without causing a fight I don't want."

"Agreed," I said. "Clint has had a lot to deal with, and he needs our support right now."

"It's been wonderful being alone with him," Nell said. "It's easy to remember why I fell in love with him. He can be very sweet."

"Clint is a good man, and he's a loved member of the family. This is what you might call a major life lesson."

"I know," said Nell. "For me, too. Give the kids hugs and kisses from us. I'll see you tomorrow. I don't know if I'll need to return to D. C., but for the next couple of days, I'll be home with you."

"That'll be great. The kids will be excited to see you."

"They told me they're having an awesome time with you, Dad, and Robbie. " That makes me so happy," Nell said, her voice wobbling a little.

"We're here for you," I said, feeling a little emotional myself.

CHAPTER NINETEEN

THE NEXT MORNING, I ROSE EARLY, INTENT ON A WALK ON the beach. I'd been thinking about Clint and Nell all night, tossing in bed with worry.

I was parking my car behind the hotel when I got a cell call from Nell.

"Hi. What's up?" I asked.

"I'm not flying to Florida today," Nell said. "I've thought about it, and Clint and I talked honestly, and I feel a lot better by staying with him while he's going through this rough time."

"I'm pleased you're doing that," I said. "I think it's the right thing to do. Use these days to support him and to make the move out of the house the easiest it can be."

"Yes, I'm going to do that," said Nell. "It's been such a tough year that I sometimes forget what our marriage was like when we first started out."

"You two have a lot of love," I told her. "That's too precious to waste."

"I'm relieved I can talk to you," said Nell. "Is everything fine at the hotel?"

"Yes, we're busy, but Lorraine is back part-time, and that helps. You and Clint should know, though, that Claudine has made a complaint to the Chamber of Commerce about Rhonda and me, as well as our hotel. We're ignoring it, but it's aggravating."

"Very much so," said Nell. "You know how I feel about Claudine."

"Rhonda and I have faced worse, but we'll keep an eye out

for any more trouble from her."

I was walking out to the beach when my cell rang again. *Vaughn.*

"Hi, what's up?" I asked him.

"I just got a call from my agent. I have to go to New York City for a couple of days. Hope you don't mind. It could mean an audition for me."

"I understand. Thank heavens for Liana. Can you do me a favor and call her to make sure she'll be on hand?"

"Okay. I'm catching a flight this afternoon. I'll give you all the details."

Vaughn ended the call, and I stepped onto the sand and walked to the water's foamy edge to stare out over the Gulf. Life was unpredictable, and I needed this peace to catch my breath. Ever since moving to Sabal, the soothing waves and the birds in the sky or scurrying along the sand brought me a peace I couldn't find elsewhere. Especially when a soft sea breeze caressed my cheeks, helping me to relax.

I'd just made it back to the hotel gate when Brock came running up to me. "Say, Ann, I heard from a friend at the Chamber of Commerce that The Beach House Hotel is about to be sued for mishandling a situation with a guest. It's something I, as the president of the Neighborhood Association, should know about. Care to comment?"

"No, Brock, I don't," I said calmly, as my pulse sprinted inside me.

I left him grumbling under his breath as I hurried through to the loading dock and into the hotel.

"Why the rush?" asked Consuela as I entered the kitchen.

"I need comfort and warmth after meeting up with Brock Goodwin," I told her, pouring myself a cup of coffee.

She gave me a grim look and handed me a plate with a warm cinnamon roll on it. "That man is beyond annoying. Did you know he tried to talk to one of Manny's gardeners about how much he was being paid? Manny told him in no uncertain terms that an employee's pay was private."

"I don't put it past Brock to do that. He can't stand not knowing more about our hotel. But much of our success is based on maintaining a sense of privacy for our guests, our staff, ourselves."

"What's going on?" asked Rhonda, coming into the kitchen. I automatically handed her a cup of coffee while Consuela loaded a plate with a sweet roll.

"I ran into Brock at the beach. I'll tell you about it later. By the way, you two, I heard from Tina Marks. She and her family will be here in a week, and she can't wait to see everyone and have some of your sweet rolls, Consuela."

Consuela beamed. "They are The Beach House Hotel's secret weapon."

Rhonda and I laughed, but it was true. They played a significant role in the hotel's early publicity.

"You've got that right, dear lady," said Rhonda.

"Love you," I added, and then walked with Rhonda to our office.

We took seats at our desks, and I faced Rhonda. "Brock told me we were being sued by someone who notified the Chamber of Commerce about us and the hotel, claiming it was unsatisfactory."

Rhonda shook her head. "No, that's not true. Someone is spreading lies. Most likely Brock. He hears something, and he builds onto the scrap of information until it's a completely different story. I'll contact my friend to see what she has to say about it."

"We don't need bad publicity when we're trying to end our year well." I shook my head. "Some days, I wonder why we seem to have so many struggles."

"If we weren't doing such an outstanding job, no one would notice us. Now, with the spotlight on our hotel, we must be prepared for attacks like this," said Rhonda. "When is Nell coming back?"

"She was going to come back today, but she's staying in D.C. to help Clint," I said. "Vaughn is leaving for New York City this afternoon for a couple of days. It's a good thing we have a contract with Liana for babysitting. It's been a little crazy at my house."

"And here at the hotel," said Rhonda. "I'm going to call my friend at the Chamber of Commerce, and then we'd better let Bernie know what's going on."

While Rhonda made the call, I returned the dishes to the kitchen and took a moment to walk through the lobby to see what was happening there.

I loved the striking difference between the holiday decorations inside and the tropical scenes outside. The smell of pine filled my nostrils as I studied the floral and pine displays inside, adding a brightness to the lobby area. But it was the large sparkling Christmas tree I loved the most, looking regal with its silver and gold theme.

Rhonda caught up to me. "There you are. My friend says there was no mention of any legal action in the complaint that she told me about. She said Brock is a nuisance at the office and we should ignore him. I told her I wished we could."

We went to Bernie's office and knocked.

He was on the phone but waved us inside.

After he ended the call, he turned to us. "What's up?"

Rhonda told him about the email the Chamber had received, and I told him about my meeting with Brock on the beach.

He listened quietly and then said, "We'll just keep on keeping on. That *dummkopf* is nothing but trouble." He turned to me. "Is Nell still out of town?"

"Yes. I don't think we can count on her for another few days. I hope you understand," I said. "Working at the hotel is very important to her, but there are details she needs to handle in D.C. to make the move here."

"As long as the hospitality department can function without her for a while, I'm okay with it," said Bernie. "But as you know, it's our busy time. I've heard that everyone likes Nell and likes working with her. It's too bad that the timing is off."

"I know," I said, wishing Nell had had a stronger beginning. Even though Rhonda and I owned the hotel and wanted family involved, Bernie was right to be concerned when a staff member was unable to work.

Following a pattern that we'd begun when we were dating, I drove Vaughn to the airport and picked him up there whenever possible. In our busy lives, it gave us a rare chance to be alone before saying goodbye or greeting his arrival back home.

"What are you auditioning for?" I asked Vaughn.

"A fairly small but important part in a movie that sounded great when my agent pitched it to me," he said. "It's a fairly short shoot schedule, and I like that more and more."

Returning his smile, I said, "Me, too."

"Thanks for all you're doing for Nell and Clint," he said. "I've purposely stayed out of a lot of discussion about it as we'd promised one another. But it's important Nell has you to talk to about it."

"I love her," I said as I pulled into the drop-off zone at the airport.

My stomach always clenched with pangs of unhappiness as I saw him off, but it also kept our marriage alive by having him leave home occasionally. The goings were sad, but the homecomings were ... well, delicious.

Vaughn kissed me, grabbed his travel bag from the back

seat, and headed into the airport wearing a baseball cap to keep people from recognizing him.

I left the airport and headed back to Sabal, thinking of the busy days ahead.

My cell phone rang. *Clint.*

"Hi, Ann. I'm going to take you up on your offer to help Nell and me. I need you to do two things for me. Are you at home?"

"Actually, I just dropped off Vaughn at the airport for a short business trip, and I'm on my way home."

"When you get there, could you please scan some papers and email them to me? I'm fairly certain it's what someone was looking for when they broke into the house. I'm still keeping the originals, which I hope you'll store in a safe place. At the moment, I've placed them in a bureau drawer, but I'm not sure they'll be okay there."

"I'll find a safe spot for them," I said. "And I'll get those copies to you."

"One more thing. I'm turning in my rental car. I've arranged for the Audi dealer in Sabal to receive it. It was nothing but an ego trip, anyway. One I'm paying for now."

Good for you, I thought. "No problem. Do you want me to keep all personal items from the car for you?"

"That would be great. The paperwork is in the glove compartment. I don't believe you'll need anything else. Nell brought both sets of openers when she drove it to Sabal."

"How are you feeling?" I asked.

"Besides feeling stupid for getting into all this?" said Clint. "Okay, I guess. The pain level is significantly lower than it was. Nell has been terrific about helping me."

"She's a special woman," I said with pride. "I'll let you know when I'm about to send the papers to you. Text me the number where you want them sent."

"Will do. And thanks," said Clint.

We ended the call, and I let out a sigh of satisfaction. Clint was sounding more like himself. I understood his desire to provide for Nell, knowing she came from money, but neither Nell nor her father ever flaunted it or demanded expensive personal possessions. That's what he should've known.

At home, I went through the bureau drawers in the guest room, where Nell and Clint were staying, and quickly found a file folder containing documents. Although I didn't want to snoop, I read enough to know which papers Clint wanted, and then I went to Vaughn's office to send them to Clint.

"Thanks," said Clint when he called.

"I'll take care of the car tomorrow," I said. "I'll get Rhonda to help me."

"That would be great," said Clint. "Talk to you then. Nell wants to say hi to you."

"Hi, sweetie. It seems to be going well," I said.

Yes, but it won't be easy for Clint to break away. I'll talk to you tomorrow. I just wanted to thank you for your help. Can I speak to the kids?"

"Sure. I'll get them," I said, carrying my phone to the lanai where they were playing a game.

Watching the children's faces light up at the news that Nell wanted to speak to them, I handed my phone to Bailey and went to talk to Liana, who'd moved into her room here at the house until further notice.

CHAPTER TWENTY

THE NEXT MORNING, BEFORE HEADING TO THE CAR dealership with Clint's car, I vacuumed the interior and made sure that all the pockets and compartments were empty of personal papers and items.

As I was going through the glove compartment, I found a note to Clint from Claudine.

"Hey, partner! I thought we'd celebrate your joining the firm and my project with a special dinner. I hope you're available because it's going to be you and me going forward. Can't wait! Xo Claudine.

I studied the note with dismay. From the very beginning, Clint had a beautiful woman enticing him to cheat. I could understand the attraction, especially if there was conflict at home. But Clint had told Claudine in front of me that there wasn't any relationship and never had been.

I tucked that note in my pocket. Though there wasn't a date on it, it might become important in any legal battle.

After everything had been removed from the car, I vacuumed and quickly spruced up the interior. I had no idea what financial arrangements had been made, but I wanted the car to look as nice as possible.

I called Rhonda, and she met me at the dealership.

After turning in the car, I climbed into Rhonda's convertible.

"Let's take a little drive," said Rhonda. "I want to go to the Chamber of Commerce and see that email from Claudine. We might need it if we receive any more harassment from her. If we end up going to our lawyer, it could be useful."

"Here. Take a look at this," I said, pulling Claudine's note out from my pocket.

Rhonda read it and shook her head. "This woman is batshit crazy. Let's see, she wants a job working for the family, wants a man, and wants her father's approval. It must have been hard never to measure up. Still, everyone knows you don't go fishing off the company pier."

"Apparently, she doesn't. As upset as I was about the prospect of Clint cheating on Nell, I'm just as upset at how Claudine pursued him from the beginning." I let out a long sigh. "It reminds me of how Kandie pursued Robert. With a lot of flattery and determination."

"The difference is your Ex fell for it. Clint didn't cross that line," said Rhonda.

"You're right. But it still bugs me when women go after married men."

"Or married men become fools thinking they can entice younger women," said Rhonda, and I knew she was remembering her ex-husband, Sal.

"A game as old as time," I grumbled.

"Let's see if we can catch this little witch at her game," Rhonda said. "She should know better than to try to hurt us or our hotel."

We drove to the Chamber, got out, and went inside to see the head of the organization. Alisa MacDonald, a charming, middle-aged woman and supporter of ours, greeted us with a smile.

"Hello to two of my favorite people," she said. "What can I do for you today?"

"I want a copy of the email and any paperwork you recorded from Claudine Everett's complaints about our hotel," said Rhonda.

"No problem. I'll forward it to you, so you can make a proper response. That's our normal procedure," Alisa said. "I wasn't sure you wanted to deal with it."

"We do," I said. "We can't let anything like that go."

"I understand," Alisa said. "We never get anything but praise for The Beach House Hotel. That's why I called you, Rhonda."

"Thanks. "Are there any other updates we should be aware of?" Rhonda asked.

"Nothing of any substance. Brock Goodwin was in here yesterday nosing around. Honestly, I find him detestable. He's selling Valentine's decorations that he wants the city to buy. I told him we weren't adding anything to our existing display."

"We turned him down, too," I said. "Let us know when you need anything from us. I see you still have our brochures on display."

"Oh, yes," said Alisa. "Excuse me. I have to take a phone call."

She left, and Rhonda and I decided to leave. A walk on the beach sounded like a relaxing way to discuss Claudine.

On the way to the hotel, I called Clint to tell him I'd delivered the car to the dealership.

"Thanks. Can't talk. I'm with my lawyer," he said.

"Good luck. I found something in the car you should know about. But it can wait until later." I ended the call.

"You know, Annie, I'm really proud of Clint for the changes he's making," said Rhonda. "I remember how sweet Nell's wedding was and how much he obviously loved her."

"Working in D.C. with powerful people can be detrimental by making you believe you deserve the same lifestyle they have. Or wanting what they have," I said.

"I have had very little money and then a lot, but you have to live your life in such a way that you can look at yourself in a mirror." Rhonda chuckled. "Although I wonder who that old lady in the mirror is. We're getting older, Annie."

"Older and wiser, I hope," I said, laughing.

At the hotel, all thoughts of personal problems were erased as Rhonda and I entered. A small fire had broken out in the kitchen. It had quickly been put out, but there was some interior damage, and Jean-Luc was in a horrible state. His kitchen was always spotless, and seeing where flames had marred a wall behind one of the stoves seemed like a personal affront to him. He'd already dismissed the new kitchen helper who'd caused the blaze.

After reassuring Jean-Luc that we'd take care of any repairs immediately, we went to our office. A holiday dinner hosted by the mayor of Sabal was on the agenda, and we needed to make sure all was in order for the event.

We walked down to the hospitality department to check with Annette on the dinner and were surprised to find Lorraine there.

Rhonda and I exchanged hugs with her.

"How's it going?" I asked her.

"It's lonelier than I thought it'd be," said Lorraine. "Arthur wasn't a large man, but he filled the house. With him gone, the house is empty, too quiet."

"Are you giving yourself enough freedom to recover?" asked Rhonda. "We love having you here, especially now that Nell is gone. But we don't want any pressure put on you to return."

"Being here is wonderful for me. It gives me something else to think about," said Lorraine. "I'm taking over for Annette today. So, I'll be handling the private dinner tonight.

Anything I should know?"

"That's why we're here," I said. "Helena Naylor is very particular about service at her dinners. While she wants everyone to be relaxed, she doesn't want too much time to elapse between courses. People tend to drink more wine than they should when that happens, and she doesn't want the mayor's office held responsible for it."

"I'm sure that won't be a problem. I'll coordinate with Jean-Luc," Lorraine said.

"I'd wait a while if I was you," said Rhonda. "There's been a small kitchen fire, and Jean-Luc is in a bad state."

"Thanks for the warning," said Lorraine. "Don't worry, though. I'll take care of the timing."

"Thanks," I said. "I'll leave it to you. If you need anything from me, you can reach me at home."

"I'm staying at the hotel a while longer, then I can be reached at home, too," said Rhonda.

We returned to our office, and I picked up my purse, ready to leave. I'd promised to pick up Ned from school for an early release day, and I didn't want to be late. Bailey was going home with Angie.

At a knock on the door, Rhonda and I both called out, "Come in!"

Bernie opened the door and walked inside, looking worried.

"What's going on?" I asked. Very little flustered Bernie, but he looked unhappy.

"The firm of Everett, Shuster, and Donnelly has hired a private detective to investigate the claims that Claudine Everett made about the hotel. He wanted to speak to you, but I told him you were unavailable, but he could talk to me. He told me he had to speak to the two of you. He gave me his business card and asked me to have you call him for an appointment."

I slammed my purse on my desk. "This is becoming a total nightmare. Why should we have to talk to him?"

"I think it's smart to clear the air with this issue," said Bernie. "But when you do talk to him, I suggest you have Mike Torson sit in. We may need a lawyer if this gets out of hand."

Rhonda stirred in her chair. "Like Annie said, this is becoming a freakin' nightmare. All because of Clint working for this firm and wanting to resign."

"It looks like they want to play hardball for some reason," said Bernie. "But for the sake of the hotel's reputation, we have to settle this issue with them."

"I agree, but I don't like it," I said. "But right now, I've got to go pick up Ned at school."

"Don't worry, Annie. "I'll work out an appointment with Mike and get back to you," said Rhonda. "But I don't like this one bit."

On the way to Ned's school, I reminded myself to calm down. I'd planned this to be a special break for Ned and me, and I didn't want to let my anger ruin that. He was a dear little boy who needed me to make our moments together pleasant.

I pulled into the line of cars in the front circle of the school and took a deep breath. I was pleased that Nell and Clint's purchase of the Wiley house would mean that Ned and Bailey would stay in the same schools they were in now.

A teacher walked her class to the front door and waited with them while they were picked up.

Ned was standing with a boy his age when he saw me. His face lit up with joy, bringing a sting of tears to my eyes. It brought back memories of Robbie.

He walked over to the car and opened the door. "Hi, Gammy!"

"Did you have a good school day?" I asked as he sat in the

back seat and buckled up.

"Yes. But I didn't eat lunch today."

"That's why I'm taking you to your favorite place," I said, smiling.

"Really? I want a burger and fries."

"Okay. That's what we'll get." I headed to the drive-through restaurant and parked the car.

Inside, after I'd ordered and received our food, I sat at a small table with Ned. He'd been pretty quiet lately, and I wanted to find out what he was thinking.

"Here you go," I said, handing him his meal and helping him get everything in place.

Sitting opposite him, I studied his smiling, alert face. He had Nell's blue eyes, and his light-brown hair was sun-streaked with blond, like hers. His features were strong like his father's, but his impish grin was his own.

"How are you liking your new school?" I asked him.

He smiled and nodded. "I have another new friend. His name is Adam."

"Making new friends is part of the excitement of moving to a new area. I'm sure you'll have many more. You already have a lot of friends if you count all your special cousins."

He gave me a serious look. "Yep. When are Daddy and Mommy coming back?"

"I'm not sure. But I wouldn't worry about them. They're getting your old house ready to sell. Then you'll have a new house in the same neighborhood as Sally Kate, the T's, and the rest of the families."

"Really? Cool." Ned grinned at me and picked up another French fry. "I like it here."

"I love having you in Sabal," I said, feeling my heart fill with love for him. My dream of having him and his family live here was coming true. I just wish it didn't involve trouble for Nell and Clint.

As if she knew I was thinking of her, my cell rang. *Nell.*

"Hi," she said. "I just remembered this was an early release day for the kids."

"Yes, Ned and I are having lunch at his favorite place," I said. "Bailey is at Angela's. Would you like to speak to Ned?"

I handed the phone to Ned and watched his face fill with pride as he told her he earned a gold star in reading. While they chatted, I ate my chicken sandwich, and then Ned handed me the phone.

"Anything new on the Claudine front?" Nell asked me.

"As a matter of fact, there is. Her company sent an investigator to check out her allegations against the hotel. Rhonda and I will meet with him and with our lawyer to make sure everything goes smoothly."

"Aw, Ann, I'm sorry you and Rhonda have become part of this mistake. That isn't fair. Clint and I would never want to put you through this."

"I know, sweetie, but we'll see it through to the end. How is it going there?"

"Smoothly with the house and the move. Bumpy for Clint, though. He has been in touch with the man who recently left the firm before him and is receiving helpful tips. But there's something off about this company. Something shady."

"Does Clint have a sharp lawyer?" I asked.

"Oh, yes. That's one thing we agreed on from the beginning," said Nell. "I've got to go. Have fun with my Ned. Tell Bailey 'hi' for me. I'll phone at bedtime."

I ended the call and turned back to Ned, hiding my frustration at the situation. One thing was for certain: Rhonda and I would fight for our hotel's reputation and do anything to help Nell and Clint.

CHAPTER TWENTY-ONE

THE NEXT DAY, AFTER THE KIDS WERE OFF TO SCHOOL AND Liana was ready to have them for the rest of the day, I headed to the hotel. Rhonda had arranged for us to meet with the investigator and Mike Torson at eleven o'clock. It would allow us time to review exactly what had happened with Claudine.

I went into the hotel kitchen to get a cup of coffee and saw Consuela. I waved and went over to her. "How are you?" I asked, giving her a quick hug.

"Fine. I've been extra busy since the kitchen fire. You know Jean-Luc doesn't like anything to go wrong with his domain."

"I do," I said. "Thank heavens there was more alarm than damage."

"Is everything all right? Rhonda is in a mood this morning," said Consuela.

"Oh, you'd better give me two sweet rolls then. We have a matter to take care of this morning, and we're both annoyed by it."

"Whatever it is, it'll be fine. You two always manage to handle any situation that arises," Consuela said in a soothing tone. She handed me a plate with two sweet rolls. "If you need to talk, I'm always here for you."

"Just knowing that makes me feel better," I said. "Thanks."

I took my coffee and treats to the office.

Rhonda was on the phone when I arrived.

She looked up at me and held up a hand. "I'm on the

phone with the state trooper who stopped us with Claudine." She took a sip of coffee. "Yes, I'm here."

I sat at my desk and opened my computer to find a message from Claudine. I opened it.

"*Sorry. The situation is now out of my hands.*"

I stared at the words and felt a ripple of unease go down my back. *What did this mean?*

Rhonda ended the call to me and said, "I've asked the state trooper if he'd be willing to testify, if necessary. He said yes, and he has the body cam footage to back up his statement. I'm not sure what is going on, but Clint's firm is out to get us."

"I just got an email from Claudine. Listen to this." I read it to her.

"It's fuckin' nonsense. We could've accused her of drugging Clint, but all he wanted was the paperwork back. You can't force someone to sign a legal paper under duress or the influence of drugs, for God's sake."

"It's a good thing Mike has agreed to be present for our meeting," I said. "After we finish our coffee, let's head out to the beach and talk it through."

"Okay by me," said Rhonda. "Thanks for the sweet roll."

"Consuela thought you might need it," I answered.

Chuckling, Rhonda said, "Guess I was in a snit earlier. I'll apologize to her."

Out on the beach, we said nothing as we faced the water, allowing sea breezes to caress our cheeks and soothe our souls. Running the hotel was more work than we'd ever imagined. But we had an excellent product and outstanding management, and we would overcome this latest obstacle.

Rhonda turned to me. "Mike Torson is aware of the Everett, Shuster, and Donnelly company. They've been questioned about a couple of shady real estate deals. Did Clint question them about it before he signed on with them?"

"I don't know, but it's something we need to ask him." I turned my back to the breeze and punched in his cell number.

He answered right away. "Hi, Ann. What's up?"

"Rhonda and I are meeting with an investigator from your company. They're questioning our behavior with Claudine. I received an email from her today, saying she's sorry, but the situation is beyond her control. Rhonda and I want to know what investigation you conducted of the company before working with them.

"I'd read about a couple of questionable deals and grilled them on it. Especially before putting in my share of equity. Nothing was proven in court, and the matter was dropped. But that's why I made my work contract with them specific. I expressed my concerns about the potential for hurting employees and others when they took over a company, and they assured me they weren't about to do that with the deals I was working on. That's why I'm pissed off."

"Can your friend testify in your favor, if necessary?" I asked.

"Yes, he had the same problem with them. Well, with Claudine mostly," said Clint. "She's great at making you feel part of the team and then changing her mind. I just want to end my association with them and recover the money I invested."

"Did the agreement state what would happen to your money if you left?" I asked.

"Yes. I was to get a major portion of it back, depending on how long I worked for them," said Clint. "My lawyer is looking over the contract."

"I'm sorry that it's come down to this for all of us," I said.

Beside me, Rhonda said, "Tell Clint we're not going to let those bastards get away with their bullshit."

"Did you hear that?" I asked Clint.

"Yes, I did. Both of you have been terrific about helping me, and I'm sorry to have dragged you into my disaster."

"How are your injuries?" I asked him.

"My right arm is doing great. My left arm will take time, but I've continued to follow the doctor's instructions. He chuckled. "Nell makes sure of it."

"I'm glad," I said. "We'll let you know how the interview goes."

I ended the call, let out a long breath, and turned to face the soothing motion of the waves once more. Clint was a decent man who'd let his ambition get him off track. It could happen to anyone. But unfortunately, he was dealing with a company that was dishonest at best.

"How is he doing overall?" asked Rhonda.

"His injuries are healing, and Nell is seeing that he follows the doctor's orders. He's very sorry to get us involved. But, as you know, all this trauma has brought Nell and Clint closer than ever."

"Yeah, my grandmother used to say when one day is dim, the next is sunny," said Rhonda. "Just think of us and the hotel."

I turned and faced her. "We can't let Clint's company ruin what we've worked for. It's a silly thing they're trying to do. I'm very relieved Mike Torson will do most of the talking for us."

"You know I'd let too many f-bombs out," said Rhonda. "Because this is driving me fucking crazy!"

I took hold of her arm. "C'mon, let's walk for a while." I looked around. "No sign of Brock. We can relax."

We were strolling along the sand when my cell phone rang. *Tina Marks.*

"Hi, Tina! Are you and your family preparing to visit us for Christmas? I asked her.

"Yes, but it'll be for fewer days than I'd wanted. Nick is

preparing to direct a movie right after the New Year, and he needs to stay in L.A. for a bit longer. I agreed to do a couple of social events with him. I'm sorry."

"Please call Bernie with the change of arrival date. Rhonda and I will spend as many hours as you can give us over the holidays. And we've already got one of the guesthouses saved for you."

"Thanks. Nick has other family, but you and Rhonda are mine," said Tina. "I can't wait to see you."

I filled Rhonda in on the news, and we turned to walk back to the hotel. I liked having these peaceful moments with Rhonda on the beach. We didn't even have to speak to understand what the other person was feeling. We'd grown that close.

Rhonda and I left our office and went to one of the smaller conference rooms to meet with Mike. He wanted a few minutes alone with us before we met with the investigator, a man named Aaron Flagg.

We entered the conference room to find Mike already seated at the head of the table. He stood when he saw us. "Ann, Rhonda, I'm glad we have a few minutes to talk before our meeting. Apparently, this was set up according to hearsay from Claudine. It's almost as if we're wasting our money on this."

Rhonda and I took seats on either side of him.

"We, along with Bernie, feel it's important to take care of this accusation before it becomes worse," I explained. "Claudine is implying that we did something illegal and refused to let her meet at the hotel, along with a number of minor complaints that seem innocuous until you add them up."

Mike listened politely, then nodded. Mike was someone who'd supported Rhonda and me from the beginning. He never disparaged anything we wanted to do and treated us with respect, even when we didn't agree. Calm, steady, and bright, he was a respected lawyer in town.

"The burden of proof will be on them," said Mike before we heard a knock on the door.

Mike got up and greeted a middle-aged man of average height and weight who stood staring at us through horned-rim glasses. His bland appearance made him seem perfect for the job.

Mike and Aaron shook hands, and then Mike made the introductions.

"I'm here representing the owners of the hotel," said Mike, indicating a chair for Aaron and sitting again at the head of the table. "Would you like to tell us why you're here?"

"My client, the firm of Everett, Shuster, and Donnelly, has asked me to investigate an incident that occurred between Claudine Everett and the owners of the hotel, Ms. Sanders and Ms. Grayson, as well as an employee working with Claudine, Clint Dawson. Apparently against her will, she was made to relinquish legal papers that Mr. Dawson had signed, enabling her to go forward with a project the company was working on."

"And how did you come by this information?" asked Mike.

"Claudine met with the partners of the company she's working for and explained the situation to them."

"Do you have proof of this happening?" asked Mike.

"Obviously, she was unable to produce the paperwork after Mr. Dawson signed it and then stole it back," said Aaron. "My understanding is that she was accosted on her return to Miami by the three people I've mentioned and forced to hand back the signed papers."

"Are you aware of where this event supposedly took place?" asked Mike.

"Somewhere along Alligator Alley, where she was driving to return to Miami," he answered.

"Are you aware that a state trooper was also at the scene?" Mike asked.

"I was told he was a friend of Ms. Grayson's. They knew one another, and he stood by while the papers were removed."

"Did she resist, refuse to do as was asked?" Mike asked.

"She said she was afraid not to do as Clint wanted because of that trooper."

Mike turned to me. "Did you sense any wrongdoing on Clint's part?"

I cleared my throat, telling myself not to let my temper show. "Claudine willingly opened her briefcase to allow Clint to remove the papers. Probably because Clint told us she had put something in his coffee during their private meeting. Rhonda and I, as well as the trooper, who was wearing his body cam, can verify that he was sick and acting out of character."

Aaron gave me a thoughtful look. "Claudine mentioned you might bring up that she'd heard from the president of the Neighborhood Association that the owners of The Beach House Hotel were always doing something just within the law to get their way."

"Are you talking about Brock Goodwin?" Rhonda asked, her voice lower than normal, and I knew she was furious.

Aaron looked at his paperwork. "Yes, that's the name she gave me."

Mike handed him a document. "I think you might want to read this. It's a detailed description of what took place alongside the highway as written by the state trooper who was involved. You and I both know he'd never perjure himself. Again, the body cam backs up his report. As it is, Ms. Sanders and Ms. Grayson could've brought charges against Claudine for the drugging incident, which they decided not to pursue as long as Mr. Dawson rightly got those papers returned."

Aaron remained quiet.

Mike handed him another sheet of paper. "This is a copy of the original agreement Mr. Dawson signed that day under false pretenses. As you can see, the signature is a weak comparison to the one on another document signed by him. I think you've wasted enough of our time."

"As Ms. Everett is a client, I'm required to do all I can to get to the bottom of this situation," said Aaron. "In this case, I agree with you. I've done what I could to clarify exactly what happened."

Aaron gathered his papers and stood.

Mike, Rhonda, and I got to our feet. Handshakes were given all around, and Aaron left.

Mike pulled his paperwork together and looked at us. "It seems a frivolous case, but I think it was wise that we made our rebuttal. We don't want the hotel's reputation smeared. Great job on getting that report from the trooper, Rhonda."

"Thanks." Rhonda winked at me.

"As always, Mike, we appreciate your support," I said.

"Before you go, tell us, what are we going to do about that jackass, Brock Goodwin?" said Rhonda.

Mike shook his head. "Unfortunately, being a thorn in someone's side isn't illegal. But don't worry. He's going to get caught for all the grief he causes others."

We walked Mike out to the lobby.

"Wait here," I said. "I've got the cinnamon rolls you've requested for your wife."

"Though we suspect they're more for you than for her," said Rhonda, letting out a roaring laugh that made Mike and me join in.

CHAPTER TWENTY-TWO

I PULLED INTO THE DRIVEWAY READY FOR A SWIM BEFORE dinner with the kids, glad the workday was over. It had been a frustrating one with a private dinner cancellation due to illness and having to juggle around waitstaff. Everyone was trying to earn as much as they could leading up to Christmas, willing to work for the extra money it would provide.

When I walked into the house, I expected to see Liana, and suddenly realized her car was gone. I called to Robbie, who ambled into the kitchen holding a can of soda. "Where's Liana? Where are Bailey and Ned?"

"Dad's here in the pool with them. He sent Liana home," said Robbie. "I'm playing a game online."

"I'll surprise them," I said, hurrying into my bedroom to change.

A few minutes later, I headed out to the pool and stopped a moment to watch Vaughn playing with the kids. Seeing him like this reminded me that he was how I, as a child, had pictured what a grandfather would be like if I'd had one.

Vaughn looked up and smiled. "C'mon in. The water's great."

"What a pleasant surprise to see you here," I said, slipping into the shallow end and letting out a gasp at the cool temperature.

He came over to me and kissed me. "I was going to call for a ride and figured you'd be too busy. Besides, I like to surprise the family. And I know Liana has been working overtime. She needs a break."

"How did the audition go?" I asked.

"Very well. There's a role for me in this new limited television series. One I'm really excited about. A caretaker falls in love with her middle-aged client."

"Sounds interesting," I said. "Who's going to play the romantic interest?"

"They're talking to Darla Delaney," said Vaughn. "That would be delightful. And with she and Meredith living part-time in Florida, it makes it easy to go over the scripts together."

"It seems like ages since we've seen them. We must include her for our post-holiday party."

"That'd be nice," said Vaughn, turning as Ned threw a blow-up football at him.

Vaughn caught it. "Okay, go out for a pass."

Ned swam into the deep end of the pool and waited for Vaughn's throw.

I joined Bailey, sitting on the steps. "How did it go at school today?"

Bailey shrugged. "I'm not part of the popular group. Some of the girls were mean to me."

Uh-oh. I put my arm around her. "You've only been here a short time. They haven't had a chance to get to know you. Not really. Give it time."

"I miss my friends back home. I miss Mom and Dad," Bailey said, snuggling closer to me.

"Life has been very chaotic," I said. "But by the beginning of the year, you'll be close to getting into your own house with your own room. With the new year, you'll have new chances to make friends. Moving to a new place can be an exciting experience. Difficult too. But in the end, it all works out."

"Thanks, Gammy. I love you," said Bailey, smiling up at me.

"Love you too." I leaned over and kissed her cheek. All

these changes hadn't been easy for her, and though I knew she'd have to handle some of the smaller frustrations on her own, I'd already decided to speak to her teacher to see what insight I could get.

Vaughn and Ned started a game of football tag, which allowed swimmers to duck under water to avoid the ball touching them.

"C'mon, girls," called Ned.

Chuckling at being included as a girl, I grabbed Bailey's hand, and we joined them.

Later, as I got out of the pool, I was relieved to see the smile on Bailey's face.

That night, as Vaughn and I snuggled in bed, I brought him up to date on the latest happenings.

"As hard as it is, it's wise for Clint to leave this company," said Vaughn. "Nothing about it sounds straightforward, and Claudine is a piece of work. To think she even brought Brock Goodwin into the picture. That's not very smart."

"You can imagine how angry that made Rhonda," I said.

Vaughn chuckled. "I can." He sobered. "I wish there was something I could do to make up for the accident to Clint. It's such a shame he's physically hurting as he goes through this process."

"I'm sure we can find something for you to do regarding the move," I said, cupping his cheek in my hand.

He took hold of it and brought it to his lips. "It's great to be home."

The next morning, I was surprised by a call from Liz. "Can you stop by my house before you head to the hotel? I want to discuss something with you. Nell, Angie, and I have come up with a plan, and we need your input and Rhonda's."

"Okay," I said. "Rhonda has agreed?"

"Yes," said Liz. "It's a bit daring, but it will be a lot of fun. You'll see when you get here."

"Okay, now you have me curious," I said, laughing. I never knew what our girls would come up with. They were a trio of creative women.

I helped Vaughn get the kids off to school, and then I headed directly to Liz's house, curious to see what plan she and the other two had come up with.

I pulled behind Rhonda's car, got out, and went inside.

Angie, Rhonda, and Liz were sitting at the kitchen bar when I walked in.

"Hi, Mom! Thanks for coming," Liz said. "I'm going to call Nell after we've had a chance to chat. Yesterday, I received a call from Hester Wiley to say they had already moved out. When their children heard about the opportunity to sell, they worked together and with an estate salesperson to empty the house. It has been cleaned from top to bottom and is in move-in condition. They called Nell to let her know that as soon as they were paid, she could take over the house."

"That's awesome! But Nell indicated that with a second mortgage on the house, she couldn't come up with the money they needed to buy the house here."

"That's where Mom comes in," said Angie. "If she would provide a swing loan, Nell could pay for the house and have control of it right away."

"That's when the fun begins," said Liz. "Nell, Angie, and I want to paint the interior rooms with the help of friends and family. People from the hotel have offered to go in on the surprise for Clint. With his injured arms, he won't be of much help."

"Aren't you getting ahead of yourself?" asked Rhonda. She crooked an eyebrow at them.

"Yes and no," said Angie, wrapping an arm around

Rhonda. "There was no point in getting excited about it if people didn't want to help out. And I was sure you'd agree to the loan. I don't ask you for much myself, but I'm happy to ask for a friend."

Rhonda hugged Angie, and dabbed at her eyes. "I'm very lucky that I'm able to do this. If I hadn't dreamed about winning the Florida Lottery, I never would have played. And now that I've won all that money, I love being able to help others. Of course, I'll lend them the money."

"Nell wouldn't allow me to ask you or Vaughn," Liz said to me.

"I understand," I said, "though we would have been pleased to do so. One thing I know is that neither Nell nor Clint would renege on a loan."

"Okay," said Liz. "Our lawyer had already drawn up the sales agreement. As soon as the funds are received at the bank, we can proceed with executing the sale. Nell is flying in this morning."

"Thanks, Mom," said Angie. "Let's go ahead and call Nell."

"One thing before you do," I said. "I know employees are trying to earn extra money for Christmas. I'm willing to pay some of Manny's workers to help with the landscaping and with painting the exterior. My treat."

"No," said Rhonda. "*Our* treat."

Liz and Angie gave one another a high-five.

"We've got the best moms in the world," said Liz.

Rhonda and I exchanged looks of satisfaction. It was such an easy, fun thing for us to do.

Liz called Nell and put her on the speaker to give her the news.

"Oh, my! Thank you! Thank you! You know we'll pay it back, Rhonda, as soon as our house sale goes through in January," said Nell. "Clint and I had a long talk about my doing this, and we'd already decided to put the house in my name only for right now because of Clint's legal fight with the company. We also agreed it was only fair for me to have the chance to work out a deal on my own. He knows it's an opportunity for the kids and us. He trusts me to handle the details. That's important to me."

"Give us the word, and Angie and I will round up some helpers," said Liz. "Mom and Rhonda are paying for the house painters and the landscaping. We're going to have a couple of painting parties with friends of ours that we'd like you to meet."

"Wow! It sounds as if you've got everything worked out," said Nell. "Rhonda, I'm going to fax you some papers, and when I get into town, I'll sign the loan agreement."

"That will work," said Rhonda. "I can easily handle the money end of it. We'll hire the lawyer to oversee the loan papers when he works on the sales agreement."

"I like that we women are able and fortunate enough to make this work with elbow grease and a lot of luck," I said.

"Thanks for everything. Love you all," said Nell. "I'll be arriving late this morning. Clint may have to stay until Christmas."

Liz ended the call, and the four of us gazed at one another.

"I love our family," said Liz. She glanced at Angie. "Meeting you as my roommate was the luckiest day ever."

"Look at what's happened to the four of us since then," said Rhonda. "It's too early for a cocktail, but how about another cup of coffee?"

"Hear! Hear!" said Angie. "And I brought Grandma DelMonte's sugar cookies."

"Oh, my! Who can resist those," I said, hugging her. I loved our family too.

CHAPTER TWENTY-THREE

BEFORE I WENT TO THE HOTEL, I DROVE BACK TO MY HOUSE to let Vaughn know about the family's plan. I hoped he wouldn't be hurt by Nell not wanting to accept money from him. It was, after all, Vaughn's financial success that was Clint's reason for going to work for a new company and investing in the project to earn more money. A little competitive, a bit immature maybe, but genuine.

Vaughn was in his office going over some paperwork when I walked in, Cindy at my heels.

"Hey, you! What are you doing here?" asked Vaughn, getting to his feet.

I went over to him for a hug and pulled up a chair. "I wanted you to hear this from me before anyone else tells you."

Vaughn listened quietly as I told him about Rhonda's loan and Nell moving into the new house earlier than planned to get the interior fixed up before Clint saw it.

"Why didn't she come to us for the money?" asked Vaughn.

"I think she wanted to keep the immediate family out of the situation," I said.

"Even though she considers Rhonda family?" Vaughn said.

"There's a bit of separation there, but yes, Rhonda's family and our own will always be closely tied," I said. "What do you think of the plan overall?"

Vaughn grinned. "I like it. It'll be a great way for everyone to show their excitement about having them live here."

"Timewise, it will work," I said. "Plans are moving really fast at this end. Nell should be arriving soon, and after all the paperwork is completed, the work on the house will begin. The home inspection has already been done. Now, we know that no major investments are needed. However, Nell wants to make a few upgrades."

My cell rang. *Liz.*

"Hi, honey. What's up?" I asked her.

"I was just leaving to pick up Nell from the airport, but I got a call from Gabe's preschool to say he isn't feeling well. They want me to come and get him right away. Will you go to the airport for Nell for me?"

"No problem. I'll be pleased to do it. It'll give me a chance to talk to her."

"Thanks, Mom. I'm disappointed it won't be me, but I need to take care of my baby."

"Of course. I'll keep in touch." I checked the time. "I'd better head out now."

"You're picking up Nell?" said Vaughn. "I'd go with you, but I have a community theater meeting to attend."

"As I told Liz, this will give me a chance to talk to Nell to see what else we can do for her."

We kissed goodbye, and I headed to Tampa.

Tears stung my eyes as I drew up to the pick-up curb and saw Nell standing there with two suitcases, looking around eagerly.

I beeped my car horn, and when she saw me, she smiled and waved.

"Surprise! I'm here to pick you up instead of Liz. Gabe isn't feeling well," I told her as I got out of the car to help her with the luggage.

"I hope it isn't serious," said Nell, hefting the larger

suitcase into the back of the SUV.

"I'm sure he'll be fine." I gave her a hug. "Welcome back to Sabal. We're very excited about your plans."

She frowned. "Dad, too?"

"He understands why you prefer doing this your way, but you know how happy he would've been to help. Between you and me, your father still feels terrible about Clint getting hurt on his boat."

"It was an accident," said Nell. "Clint knows that."

At the sight of a policeman approaching us, we both jumped into the car, and I pulled away from the curb.

I glanced at Nell. "It's going to be fun to have everyone work on your house. It'll take a team to get everything done in the short period we have before Christmas and Clint's return to Sabal."

"I hope he's going to be pleased with the changes," Nell said, her eyes sparkling with excitement. "We haven't discussed exactly what I have in mind. He thinks I'm only going to do a couple of things to prepare the house for the move. Frankly, he doesn't want to worry about them."

"Let's get some lunch," I said. "Would you like to go to the hotel or another place?"

Nell shook her head. "I want to go directly to Home Depot. I have colors in my mind for the bedrooms and the main areas, and I need to pick up paint samples. Plus, Liz told me that I'll want some new light fixtures. I thought I'd look for them there and at another place I know."

"Okay. That sounds like fun. I understand you're due to meet with Hester and Earl Wiley late this afternoon."

"That's right. Before then, I'll meet with Rhonda and the bank. So, it will be a busy afternoon. I have no time to waste."

I gave her a mock salute. "I'm at your service."

She laughed. "Thanks, Ann. I love that you're always willing to support me."

"You're my daughter," I said.

Nell's eyes teared up. "I'm very grateful to you. This has been a rough time."

"Your father and I are sorry you couldn't talk to us before now," I said. Vaughn would do anything for his children and Liz.

"Clint and I are adults with a family of our own. I felt as if we should be able to work it out for ourselves. But now, I understand the value of a family's support. Liz has organized everything for buying the house."

"You two are the closest of sisters. That's very touching to me."

"Me, too," said Nell, chuckling even as she held back tears.

We walked inside the store and went directly to the paint section, where a wall was filled with paint samples available for people to take.

"I know pretty much what I want," said Nell. "According to the photos that Liz sent, I've chosen bedrooms for the kids. For Bailey's room, I'm looking for a soft peach color. Instead of a traditional blue for Ned's room, I'm going for a green with blue tones, if that makes sense."

"What about the master bedroom?"

"I'm thinking a very soft, buttery tone," said Nell.

"And the main part of the house?" I asked, impressed by how much Nell had thought about the interior.

"A white that isn't too stark," said Nell.

We stood gazing at the samples. Whenever I saw something that I thought Nell might like, I took the sample card. A few times, when I showed my choices to her, she'd picked out the same one.

"Okay, I've got what I need," said Nell. "Let's look at lights and fans. I'll take pictures of the ones I think might work."

I loved looking at different possibilities and waited while Nell took photos of the ones she liked.

When she was through, she turned to me. "Can we make one more quick stop?"

"Sure," I said. "Where?"

"To the lighting store down the street," Nell answered.

"Okay, then we'd better get some lunch. It's going to be a long day for you."

"Thanks. That sounds lovely."

The visit to the lighting store was a lot more time-consuming than we'd thought. The number of choices meant that the selection process was slow.

We left the store, and realizing it was late, we decided to go to a drive-thru location to grab some lunch before heading to my house so Nell could pick up her car.

"I hate not seeing the kids when they come home from school, but I have to take care of business. I'll surprise them later."

"They'll be thrilled to see you. They'll understand, especially when they see the house and realize it's in the same neighborhood as their other family members," I said. "I'll drop you off, and then I have to go to the hotel."

"Thanks for everything," said Nell. "I'll see you tonight."

After dropping off Nell at my house, I drove to the hotel to make sure the three in-house functions were set for tonight. A dinner in the private dining room was scheduled along with a small event in the library and a special holiday cocktail party by the pool lanai.

Grateful that Lorraine had declared it was best for her to be at the hotel instead of moping at home, I parked the car behind the hotel and went inside.

"How's everything with Nell?" Rhonda asked me as I sat down at my desk in our office.

I filled her in and then said, "Is everything going smoothly here?"

"The ladies' luncheon was a big success, but one of the toilets got clogged and we had to call in a plumber, which made it a little inconvenient for the attendees. I know we usually wait until it's quieter in the day to do our repairs, but we couldn't this time."

"No problem. Those public restrooms get a workout with all the parties," I said. "What else is going on?"

"Annette is handling the coordination of staff for each event, and she's a bit frantic because some of the younger, part-time staffers have left Florida to go home for the holidays."

"It's difficult at this time of year. That's for sure. Are we giving bonuses to those who do a double shift?" I asked. We'd discussed it but hadn't decided how we wanted to handle it.

"I told Annette to go ahead and offer it to dining room staffers," said Rhonda. "Let's check on Lorraine and see how she's doing."

We walked to the hospitality department. Annette, Lauren, and Lorraine were gathered around Annette's desk.

"Hello. How's everything going?" I asked.

Lorraine looked up and frowned. "Usual holiday problems. With cancellations in one group or another, we have to make sure that the guaranteed number of attendees is met for billing purposes."

"There's a lot of illness," said Lauren. "But we have some flexibility according to the quotes we gave for the function."

"I'm working on staffing," said Annette. "By offering bonuses to some, I think I've got the events covered. We'll be a little short in the dining room, but not enough to be a significant problem."

"Thank you, everyone," said Rhonda.

"We appreciate all your hard work," I said.

"I'd rather be busy like this," said Lauren. "A friend of mine works at another hotel, and they're not that full. Then, of course, they're not The Beach House Hotel."

Grinning, I turned to Lorraine. "How are you doing? Is it too much for you right now?"

Lorraine shook her head. "Being active here is a blessing for me. I'm still adjusting to being alone." Tears pooled in her eyes. "Arthur filled my life in such a beautiful way."

CHAPTER TWENTY-FOUR

SEVERAL DAYS LATER, I STOOD IN THE UPSTAIRS ROOM designated for Bailey with a paint roller in my hand. I, like others before me, was helping with the transformation of the interior of Nell's new house. The exterior had already been painted a light beige, and Nell had chosen a deep turquoise for the front door, a pretty tropical color.

I was working under the instruction of one of the professional painters whom Rhonda and I had hired to oversee the work. Bailey's room walls were to be coated with a shade of peach called Glee. Being part of Nell's project had become a show of unity among the hotel employees. The process was moving quickly and needed the constant guidance of the professional whose boss was a cousin of Manny's.

"Okay, you know how to put paint on the roller. Now, be careful to roll it on the wall evenly to get a smooth color effect on the walls," said my coach, an encouraging young man working for his uncle.

After a few unsure attempts, I worked easily, covering up the old pink walls and giving them an entirely new and fresh look. A member of the hotel staff joined me, and we worked together to do the job. We were to leave the wall near the ceiling alone, so the paint didn't get on the ceiling. The professionals not only prepared and taped the walls for painting, but they also put the finishing touches on each of the rooms.

A couple of hours later, I stood rubbing my back and

staring with pride at the room.

Vaughn, who had been assigned Ned's room, came up behind me. "Are you sore?"

I laughed and turned to him. "I've discovered muscles I didn't know I had. Are you done with Ned's room?"

"Yes, and we've started on the guest room. I'm pleased with the house's structure. It's sound. It may have needed dressing up, but that's all."

I walked with him to Ned's room and looked inside. The dark green color on the walls was the one both Nell and I liked best, and it was perfect for a boy's room.

We moved to the guest room/office, and I loved the soft, gold-colored walls. Though the main part of the house downstairs would become a warm white, the rooms upstairs each had their distinct flavor.

"Thanks, everyone," I called as I went down the stairs. I had to get home and change to go to the hotel. We were, as usual, extra busy during this holiday.

On my way out, Rhonda and Will arrived. We all wanted to do our share to help. It had become a family thing.

"The hotel is fine," Rhonda told me. "We heard from the private investigator that the issue with the hotel and Claudine has been resolved." Her lips curled. "I think he was embarrassed when he realized she'd left out a lot of important details in her story."

"From what Nell tells me, Clint's company is trying to enforce a non-compete clause even though any job he gets through Will and Reggie isn't at all like his work for Everett, Shuster, and Donnelly. I wonder how they can be that mean and spiteful. I know people can be that way, but it seems senseless."

"I agree," Rhonda said. "Say hi to Tina for me. I'll see her this afternoon when we get together for a champagne toast."

"Will do," I said, excited to see Tina and her boys.

Nicholas was going to fly to Sabal in a couple of days.

After changing at home, I drove to the hotel, geared up for the day. Thankfully, no weddings were scheduled. That was the last thing we needed when we were all working hard on Nell's house and continuing to provide excellent service at the hotel.

Nell's project had generated a lot of camaraderie among our staff members. Most of all, Angie, Liz, and Nell had become even closer. They worked together to choose light fixtures and to decide on small details that made a house a home.

At the hotel, I walked into the kitchen to greet Consuela and grab a cup of coffee. I didn't need a sweet roll. Consuela had sent a huge tray of cinnamon rolls to Nell's house for the crew members working there.

"Hi," I said, pouring my coffee and turning to her. "How's it going here?"

"Busy. Our customers like holiday coffee parties. The dining room has been full of them taking the place of luncheons that were sold out." She wiped her forehead. "I've been busy."

I put an arm around her shoulder and gave her a squeeze. "You are such a treasure. And everyone loves what you do. The cinnamon rolls are the best. Thanks for sending some to Nell's house. It's the perfect thing for a break."

Consuela smiled at me. "It looks like someone has been working there." She reached up and tugged on some strands of hair.

I laughed. "I'm sore, but at every stroke I took to cover up the ugly old paint, I felt terrific."

"It's great how everyone is pitching in. That's because you and Rhonda have made us a family," said Consuela. She lifted her hand and patted my cheek.

"I blinked away tears. "I guess I'd better get to the office. Rhonda and Will are at the house ready to paint. See you later. Thanks."

At the hotel, I checked for messages, and after taking care of them, I headed to the library. A popular women's club in the area had reserved the room to hold an afternoon tea for the benefit of a women's shelter. It was an event that Rhonda and I were excited to have in the hotel.

I opened the door to the library, went inside, and stood a moment to admire the festive décor. Tables of four, covered in dark green linen, filled the room. Atop each table sat a crystal bud vase filled with holiday greens and a single, beautiful red rose. A large arrangement of greens and a variety of flowers sat on the small dais at the end of the room. A microphone was already in place.

Annette came up behind me. "Pretty, huh?"

"Very. Simple but beautiful," I responded. "I love this event. For every guest seated, a donation of $100 is made to our charity."

"I like the idea of women helping women," said Annette. "We've just finished setting up the private dining room for the Livingston family group. Want to see?"

We went to the private dining room, and the setting was much more formal. A long table filled the center of the room. Crystal glassware, sparkling silverware, and holiday gold-rimmed dishes were part of the display. The arrangement in the center of the table was filled with greens, gold balls, and orchids. Though it was very different from the library's decorations, it suited the style and mood of this elegant room.

"Is the dining room prepared for this dinner?" I asked Annette.

"Yes. All the food ordered has been delivered, including

the lobster tails," Annette said. "It's such a lovely way for the family to get together each year."

"Especially as Mr. and Mrs. Livingston age," I said. Elderly now, the Livingstons were one of my favorite couples. They quietly insisted on the best, making it a challenge for us and the staff to produce a delicious meal with stellar service.

I left Annette and returned to the office to make sure the billing was prepared for the Livingston dinner. Later, I would greet the women at tea before making sure that the guesthouse Tina had rented was ready for her arrival.

After leaving the women enjoying their tea, I walked over to the guesthouses and let myself into the one Tina had rented. Stepping inside, my excitement grew, knowing Tina and her two boys would soon be there. Rhonda and I hadn't opened the hotel for long before a Hollywood agent called to ask for our help hiding Tina while she lost some weight before starting a new movie. She'd been a total brat when she'd first arrived at the hotel. Now, she was like a daughter to me and Rhonda.

I heard the sound of a car outside and, surprised, went to see who it was. At the sight of Tina and her sons getting out of a white limousine, I ran to her.

"Ann! It's great to see you!" Tina wrapped her arms around me, and we rocked back and forth.

"Mom, can we go inside? I want to go for a swim," said Victor, her oldest son, who was the same age as Bailey.

"Better give Aunt Annie a hug first," said Tina.

I hugged Victor and then his younger brother, Tyler.

The limo driver carried the suitcases inside the front door.

While Tina took care of tipping him, I went inside to check on the boys.

I saw a pile of clothes in the middle of the living room and heard them outside, where I went to check on them.

They were in the shallow end of the pool, laughing and splashing at one another.

"That was fast," I said. "I bet that feels delightful after your flight."

"It does," said Victor. "We wore our swimsuits under our clothes. Mom says we can get together with all the kids. Where are they?"

"Most of them are in school. But there will be plenty of chances for you to see them."

Tina came out on the lanai. "How does that feel?"

"Great, Mom," said Victor. "Auntie Ann says we'll get to see all the kids."

"They're almost out of school for vacation, and we've planned a lot of get-togethers. I'll leave you to get settled here, then Rhonda and I will come back to celebrate with you. Rhonda has a special bottle of champagne for us to share. A homecoming for the 'daughter' we love."

Tina clapped her hands together. "That sounds lovely."

She hugged me goodbye, and I left to check the progress at Nell's house before returning to the hotel. I hadn't mentioned it to Tina yet, but I hoped she'd do a little work on the house because it had become a family affair.

I arrived to discover a number of cars parked in front of Nell's house. It was satisfying to see that many. It meant that work inside was being done at lightning speed.

When I walked inside the house, all was quiet except for the music blaring from a well-placed phone. Several people were painting the main floor rooms. I climbed the stairs. The rooms on the second floor had all been painted except for trim work. Even though Nell wanted to completely redo the upstairs bathrooms, she knew that was something that would have to wait.

The complementary colors and the freshness of the paint gave the second floor a whole new feel.

"It looks nice, huh?" one of the professional painters said to me, paintbrush in hand.

"Such a difference," I said.

"We'll do the trim tomorrow," he said. "And then it'll look even better."

"Thanks for your help. This work couldn't be done without you."

"We have plenty of people working on it. The downstairs is coming along, too," he said.

I followed him down the stairs and went to check out the main bedroom suite.

A buttery white was being painted on the walls. I studied it and approved. It was a perfect backdrop for any bedding Nell might choose.

Nell came over to me. "Like it?"

"I do," I said. "Everything looks nice and fresh. I'm excited that Clint will see this version of the house instead of the original. I know he was proud to have that big house of yours in Maryland."

"It makes a lot more sense for us to live in this one," said Nell. "It's already more like home to me than the one he chose."

"It's a great neighborhood for kids," I said. "Families of all sizes."

"He's going to love having Reggie and Chad nearby," Nell said. "His mother isn't close with us at all."

"How's he doing with the business settlement?" I asked her.

Nell shrugged. "I think the company is realizing they can't hold him back from doing anything else, and that they went against their word in dealing with him the way they did."

"It sounds hopeful," I said.

"I think so, too. More than that, Clint is healing well. What seemed like a disaster some weeks ago now seems manageable. He's anxious to come here, but he's going to supervise the shipping of our remaining furniture from our house there, and then he'll fly here for Christmas. His lawyer said that at this stage, there's no reason he has to stay up north."

"I'm relieved. Has Vaughn gone to pick up the kids from school?"

"Yes," said Nell. "I explained to him that I don't want the kids here while we're in the middle of transitioning the house. When the painting is done, they can come and help with a small project to feel part of it. If they see too much, they're bound to give away my secret to Clint."

I laughed. "The other day, Bailey was trying her best not to tell me what she made me for Christmas. It was adorable. She knows no matter what it is, I'll love it."

Nell smiled. "I have to pick up something special for each child's room, and I want them to help me choose. The rest of their belongings have been packed and will be sent along with the furniture, but it's gratifying for them to have a fresh start."

I put my arm around her. "That's exactly what you and Clint are doing—giving yourselves a fresh start."

CHAPTER TWENTY-FIVE

RHONDA AND I SAT WITH TINA ON THE BEACH IN FRONT OF the guesthouse, watching Victor and Tyler playing with Bailey and Ned on the sand.

"It's fantastic being here," said Tina. "It really is the home of my heart with the two of you, enjoying some bubbly together. It makes our holidays full."

"You don't mind missing all those glamorous Hollywood parties?" teased Rhonda.

Tina shook her head. "No. This is real." She turned to me. "Your old friend, Lily Dorio, just got divorced from her husband. He's a really nice guy. Their marriage lasted longer than I thought it would."

I remained quiet. Lily Dorio had once tried to split up Vaughn and me.

"That woman is a disaster," said Rhonda. "Not worth a worry."

"Agreed," I said. "What else is new in your area?"

Tina told us about new movies and series that were coming out.

We listened and asked a few questions, interested, as always, in learning about Tina's life.

"Your boys are growing fast," I commented. "Any more thoughts of buying a vacation place in Sabal?"

Tina smiled wistfully. "You know how much I'd love that. Nick isn't ready for it. But as we know, time goes by fast, and living here is still a dream of mine."

"Annie just likes to keep family close," said Rhonda,

giving me an understanding look.

"You still can't convince Ty that he and June should move here?" Tina asked me.

I shook my head. "June has such a big family in San Francisco that I don't think it will ever happen. Her grandmother is the matriarch of it, and she wants her grandchildren to appreciate and be part of the Asian community there."

"Well, I know it's a big deal to have Nell here at last," said Tina.

"You should see the house Liz and Angie found for her in their neighborhood," said Rhonda. "It's perfect."

"Or will be," I said. "Painting walls and making a few changes has made such a difference. Doing the work on it has become a community affair for the hotel staff. I'm sure there's something you can do there."

"Aw, that's very sweet. Of course, I want to help," said Tina. "Tell me more."

Rhonda and I took turns telling her about the house and everything that was being done to it.

"By the time Clint arrives, the basic work should be done. Until their legal matters are settled, they won't know what other upgrades they can do to the house," I explained.

"Manny is working on the landscaping tomorrow, then we're pretty well done outside," I said. "I'll take you there tomorrow."

"Great. I think I'll talk to Manny to see if I can help plant flowers. That's something I can do," said Tina.

My lips curved, pleased she wanted to participate.

Rhonda lifted her tulip glass of champagne. "Here's to us. May we always be family."

"Yes, family. My family," I said, thinking back to my lonely childhood as I watched some of our children play together.

###

The next day, Tina arranged to meet Rhonda and me at Nell's house to see the project for herself. When we arrived, she was working with Manny planting flowers in two beautiful turquoise pots positioned on either side of the front door.

Tina looked up as we walked toward them. "I thought this would be an attractive touch."

"The pots are gorgeous," I said. "And I love the Gerbera daisies."

"Manny, you've done a great job with the landscaping," said Rhonda. She stood back and gazed at the house. "It's a whole different look."

"I love it," I said. "This has been such a beautiful example of people working together to get things done. The girls are going to take care of a few decorating touches inside, and then it will be ready for Clint to see."

"None too soon," said Tina. "When I spoke with her, Nell told me he's coming home tomorrow, a little sooner than she'd thought."

We walked inside the house. Painters were conducting an inspection, touching up missed spots, and making sure everything was completed.

We went through the house. The upstairs rooms had had new carpeting installed, which made the rooms look even better.

As we were about to leave, Nell showed up with Angie and Liz, carrying Gabe.

When he saw me, Gabe held out his arms. I pulled him into mine, well aware of how fast even this baby of the family was growing.

"The carpeting people are due to arrive to replace the one in the main bedroom downstairs," said Nell, sounding breathless as she and Angie carried bags into the house. "Manny has agreed to install some new fixtures for us."

Manny grinned as Nell set down her packages and gave Manny a pat on the back.

"We'll leave you to it," said Rhonda.

"I understand Clint will be returning to Sabal tomorrow. Any idea what time?" I asked Nell.

"He's on the eleven o'clock flight," said Nell. "I'm going to pick him up and bring him to the house. I thought we'd have lunch here. Why don't the three of you join us? It'll be a small celebration. After the first of the year, when we're settled in the house, I'm going to host a big party for everyone who's helped transform it."

"That sounds like fun. And the three of us will be here at noon tomorrow for the big reveal," I said, silently confirming that with Rhonda and Tina, who nodded their approval.

"Do you want me to take Gabe?" I asked Liz.

"No, thanks. Liana is watching him while the Ts are in school," said Liz.

"That's nice," I said. "She's been wonderful about helping out."

"I've got to get back to my boys," said Tina. "I hired one of the hotel's babysitters to watch them, but she's new to me, and I don't want to leave them with her for too long."

"All the babysitters that the hotel recommends are excellent," said Rhonda. "But I understand." She checked her watch. "Guess we need to go too. Annie and I have a meeting to attend."

At the hotel, Annette, Bernie, Lorraine, Jean-Luc, and the department heads met in a boardroom to discuss staffing for the Christmas and New Year's holidays. We made an effort to make it easy for employees to spend time with their families.

The schedule had already been set up. Now, we needed to reconfirm. Rhonda and I always accommodated our families during the holidays, even if it meant being on call at home.

Bernie and Annette usually took off after the holidays to take a short trip somewhere away from Sabal. The rest of the department heads waited until after the holidays to enjoy some personal time. However, in the hotel business, the work of operating it never truly ended.

When Bernie was satisfied that we were well-staffed for the next three weeks, he broke apart the meeting. Rhonda and I stayed behind to discuss bonuses for certain employees.

"How's Nell doing? Is she expected to return to work as you mentioned? Or should we give her a little more time?" he asked me.

"She's planning on coming back as soon as the kids return to school the first week in January. It's important to her. You've been very flexible. I appreciate it," I said.

"We both do," added Rhonda.

"I didn't want to put you on the spot in front of the others," Bernie said. "High season will be in full gear when she returns, and we need to be able to count on her."

I made a mental note to speak to Nell about the commitment. Liana had agreed to continue to help with the kids in exchange for college tuition and expenses—a plan she and Vaughn had devised. Nell was the first of our daughters to decide to work at the hotel. Something her husband and children would have to get used to.

CHAPTER TWENTY-SIX

The next day, what was supposed to be a low-key welcome home party for Clint, turned into something much bigger. Vaughn, Will, and Reggie joined Angie, Liz, Tina, Rhonda, and me for a luncheon I had catered by the hotel. The men had worked as hard as the women in getting the house ready, and it seemed only right to include them.

We gathered in the empty kitchen, waiting to rush out front to surprise them as soon as we heard Nell's car in the driveway.

I gazed around the room, feeling as if the empty house was already a home because of the love that had gone into changing it. Vaughn caught my eye and winked, understanding what I might be feeling.

The sound of a car in the driveway brought us out of the kitchen and onto the front walk just as Clint awkwardly emerged from the car. His eyes were round with surprise as he gazed from us to the house and back again.

"Welcome home," said Liz.

"Welcome to your new house," Angie added.

Nell came up beside Clint, and as she reached for his arm, he turned away from her and us.

It wasn't until I saw his shoulders shaking that I realized he was crying. My own eyes stung with tears. Clint had been on an emotional roller coaster since Thanksgiving.

"Wow!" said Clint, facing us once more. "This is great! What a change from the original photos. I can't believe it."

"C'mon inside," said Nell. "I can't wait to show you what

our family and other people have done to have this house ready for you. For us."

"We've got champagne," said Rhonda. "Show him around, and then we're going to celebrate."

While Nell took Clint on a quick tour, Rhonda popped open a bottle of champagne, and Will opened another. Vaughn and I arranged the food on the kitchen bar and waited with the others for Clint and Nell to return.

Clint's face was as flushed as Nell's when they walked into the kitchen. Their red-rimmed eyes told a story of their own. But their smiles met ours. We'd done it. We'd completely surprised Clint, who was still wearing casts or removable splints on his arms. There's no way he could've done the work that we accomplished for him.

"Thank you, everyone, for all your contributions. Sorry to be emotional, but it's been a rough time. Having you here and showing us this kind of support makes all the difference."

"Let's make a toast to that," said Vaughn, handing him a plastic tulip glass full of champagne and one to Nell.

After we all had been served, we lifted our glasses in the air. "Here's to family!" I said.

Cries of "Hear! Hear!" followed, and then we dug into the food.

After lunch, Rhonda and I spoke alone about the welcome home for Clint.

"I've always been fond of Clint," said Rhonda. "But when I saw his tears at seeing his house and us standing there, I loved him more than ever."

"He can be pretty quiet," I said. "But seeing his reaction meant a lot to me. It's been tough on those kids. Parents want their children to be happy and settled. I feel as if Nell and Clint are back on track now."

"Will tells me that Clint is going to work with him for a few weeks as a test period. If it goes well, he and Reggie will ask him to be a partner." Rhonda shook her head. "There's no way they'd even test him if they weren't sure about him."

"That's one area I'm definitely staying away from. But I hope it all works out."

Rhonda winked at me. "It was just you, me, Liz, and Angie not that long ago. Look what's happened to us."

I grinned. "I love having Tina and her family included for the holidays. There's always room for more."

"Always," Rhonda agreed before we headed to the private dining room to check on the preparations there.

At home, my house was filled with the excited sounds of Ned and Bailey on the lanai talking to their dad about their activities. Vaughn and Robbie were on the dock.

I walked to the guest room to check on Nell.

She was on the phone and waved me inside the room.

I lowered myself onto the lounge chair and waited for her to finish, pleased to have this moment to relax.

She ended the call and turned to me. "The new furniture won't be delivered until after Christmas. But the moving company has reconfirmed delivery for December 27th, which means Clint and I, and the kids can start the new year in our own home." She clasped her hands and let out a sigh. "This whole month has seemed as if we've had one miracle occur after another to make a move here possible. There's no way any of this would've happened without you and Dad and Rhonda and the rest of the family." She chuckled as she took a seat on the lounge beside me. "I think Clint is in a state of shock at how fast everything is changing."

"Did you take the kids to see the house when you and Clint went back to look at it again?" I asked.

"Yes. They're thrilled with their new rooms. Clint and I

noted what else we wanted to add to the function and décor. I think he would've been very discouraged if he'd seen it as the Wileys had it. Everything looks clean and fresh and welcoming."

"It's a beautiful home," I said.

"We're lucky to have it," Nell said. "I have a feeling the money Clint gave the company won't be returned for some time. They can't keep it forever, but they can make it difficult for us. I don't want to borrow any more money after we pay off Rhonda. We've both learned a lot of lessons from this past year," said Nell, and let out a little sigh. "More lessons to come, I'm sure. Clint and the kids will have to get used to my working at the hotel. It's too important to me."

"You're lucky to have outside help to make it less stressful for them."

Nell sat up straighter. "I know I'm luckier than most, and I appreciate that. But, Ann, I believe every woman has the right to grow and expand beyond her personal experiences, even when she has a family. I understand it's difficult for some to do that, but the idea that she's not entitled to do so is scary to me."

"Me, too," I said. "But each woman must decide how best to handle what they've been given. For many, choice is taken away by circumstances and sometimes even brute force."

"Are you talking about abuse?" asked Nell.

"Physical and emotional abuse. Even ordinary control by others. Maybe something as simple as trying to meet the expectations of the people around her." I realized how different it was today from when I was growing up with my grandmother.

"Do you think Liz and Angie mind that I'm working at the hotel when they're not ready to do so?" asked Nell.

I wrapped an arm around her. "Not at all. You're the oldest of our three daughters. Rhonda and I are delighted. The time will come when the three of you will be responsible for the hotel. You can start."

"Thanks. That makes me happy," Nell said, and rising together, we went to be with the rest of the family.

The next day, Tina's husband, Nicholas Swain, arrived. A well-known Hollywood director, he and Vaughn were friends. After meeting in the afternoon, Vaughn agreed to take him sailing in the morning.

At dinner, Vaughn shared his plans with us.

Clint surprised everyone by asking if he could go too. "I need to be on board to overcome any fear I have. I promise to stay in the cockpit the entire time."

"Okay. Robbie is going, too," said Vaughn. "We'll all keep an eye on you."

"Thanks," said Clint. He grinned at Vaughn, but I could tell that Nell was worried. She glanced at me, and I remained silent. His right arm and lower left arm were almost healed. His upper left arm, however, was still in a cast.

"Robbie, sweet brother, I'll depend on you to help Clint," said Nell, ruffling his hair as he sat beside her.

"I will," Robbie said earnestly, and I wanted to hug him.

"The weather is supposed to be nice," said Vaughn. "Warm and gentle sea breezes."

"I'll be fine," said Clint. "I need this."

Nell studied him, and the issue was settled.

The next morning, I decided to take a walk on the beach. I loved having my family around, but I relished a few quiet moments to myself. I quietly dressed and left the house while everyone was still sleeping.

As I drove to the hotel, the rising sun was spreading pink fingers through the gray morning sky. I knew they would be met with orange and yellow colors as the day grew lighter.

Sunsets and sunrises along the Gulf Coast drew the attention of visitors and locals alike.

After I parked the car at the hotel, I walked onto the beach and sprinted over to the hard-packed sand near the water's edge. Still in sneakers, I began to jog along the shore, grateful for the movement. As busy as we sometimes were, my physical activity was sometimes lacking.

I jogged a distance from the guesthouses and then turned around to go back. As I came closer, I realized the couple I had seen talking together in the distance was Tina and Brock Goodwin.

My steps slowed. I wanted nothing to do with Brock after he'd inserted himself in the investigation concerning Claudine.

Brock noticed me and waved me forward.

Trying to control my temper, I walked over to them.

"'Morning, Tina. I didn't expect to see you up this early," I said.

"I couldn't sleep. Brock saw me," Tina said tersely. She, too, was not a fan of Brock's.

"I thought she might introduce me to her husband. I could offer him a real bargain on supplies and props needed for his movies," Brock said smugly.

"The studio has people who are responsible for that," Tina said.

"Don't you ever stop trying to swindle people with your products?" I asked, burning with anger. Rhonda and I had asked him many times not to try to sell his wares to our guests. Actually, we didn't want him to speak to them at all, but that was impossible to control.

"I don't know what you mean, Ann. My imports are of high quality," huffed Brock.

"So, you say. You know, Brock, that Rhonda and I are

aware of how you became involved in a recent investigation with one of our guests. You should have nothing to do with it, as they were staying at our hotel."

"Do you mean Claudine Everett? She was all over me, asking me questions. She'd even agreed to go out with me," Brock said haughtily.

"Figures," I said.

Tina came to my side and put an arm around me. "Look, Brock, I'm well aware of what kind of man you are and will not mention your proposal to my husband. Like Ann says, I know what kind of man you are. I'll never forget the slimy way you treated me when I was a lonely, unhappy teenager."

Brock glared at us. "You women want to keep bringing up old stuff. Move on."

"Time for *you* to move on," I said.

Tina and I headed toward her guesthouse together.

"Insufferable man," groused Tina. "Let's have a cup of coffee on the lanai before you have to get to the hotel."

We went inside. Tina poured us each a cup of coffee, and we went out to the lanai. I'd often wished for mornings like this with her and sat back in one of the chairs, relishing this quiet moment with her.

At the sound of little footsteps, we turned and saw Victor and Ty in their pajamas.

I held out my arms, and Tyler went into them while Victor climbed up on the lounge chair next to his mother.

Cuddling Tyler, I thought it wouldn't be too much longer before he'd feel too old for this. He was a sweet little boy, much quieter than his brother.

When I knew I couldn't stay any longer, I reluctantly got to my feet.

Nicholas entered the lanai and waved at us before kissing Tina. "It's going to be a great day for sailing. I can't wait."

I explained that Clint would be joining them.

Nicholas lifted his eyebrows in surprise. "Brave man."

"He's determined to get back on the boat to chase away any bad memories," I said. 'I'm glad you men will be together to enjoy the sea breezes."

Tina and I hugged goodbye, and I left, pleased that Tina had such a lovely family.

CHAPTER TWENTY-SEVEN

THAT AFTERNOON, WHILE VAUGHN, NICK, AND CLINT were out on the boat, I took a few hours off to meet with Nell and Tina for a little Christmas shopping. I liked to give local businesses my attention and shopped for Christmas throughout the year at the stores in Sabal and elsewhere along the coast.

Tina's boys were at Rhonda's house with her kids. Bailey and Ned were at Liz's house. So, with a sense of freedom and fun, the three of us enjoyed walking around downtown. We ended up at André's, our favorite place for lunch.

Even though Margo Durant, one of the owners, sat us at a private corner table, a few fellow diners recognized Tina but, thankfully, didn't ask for autographs. The people in Sabal were growing more comfortable with celebrities, which made it much easier for Vaughn and me to relax in town.

"With everything else that's been going on, I haven't done much holiday shopping," said Nell. "I've been able to order some presents online, but that isn't the same as walking into a local store to get what I want."

"I've had a few items sent to your house," said Tina. "But we in my family don't do too much for ourselves for Christmas, other than taking advantage of travel opportunities."

I finished my quiche and checked my watch. "It's no problem to have packages sent or stored at our house. Robbie knows to stay away from my dressing room during the holidays, and I've told the same thing to Bailey and Ned."

"Thanks for lunch," said Tina as I rose.

"It was delicious," Nell said.

I left and hurried back to the hotel to handle a private late luncheon for the mayor. She was entertaining her staff members and special guests with a holiday celebration as a gesture of thanks for their continued support.

At the hotel, I met Lauren in the private dining room as the mayor arrived. "As usual, everything looks lovely. Thank you."

Helena Naylor was a friend of Rhonda's and mine, and I was delighted to arrange this luncheon reservation for her.

As her guests began to arrive, I left Lauren in charge and went to the hospitality office to check on the progress there. Several years ago, we'd initiated some unique arrangements for guests staying at the hotel for Christmas Eve. This year, we'd continue the practice of providing gifts for our guests, along with cocoa, cookies, and notes for Santa. Some guests even sent personal, private gifts ahead to be delivered to their rooms late on Christmas Eve. It was a lot of extra work for our employees, but it was worth the effort because we sold out early.

I walked into the office to find Dorothy Stern and her friends wrapping gifts for the guests. This year, we stuck to the gold and silver theme the decorator had chosen for us. As we did for some fundraisers, we allowed certain shops in town to include stocking gifts along with ours. It was a smart way for them to introduce their products, and it helped fill our gift boxes.

I went over to Dorothy and hugged her. "I'm glad to see you. Thanks for your help." I recognized her two friends and spoke to them. "Have you ordered lunch from the dining room?"

"Oh, yes," said one of the women. "Dorothy made those arrangements for us."

Through thick glasses, Dorothy's eyes twinkled. "We even tasted a special holiday dessert that will be served this evening."

Chuckling, I said, "I'll check on you later."

As I walked back to the office, I saw Bernie and waved. I was tickled to see the red tie he was wearing. No doubt, Annette had chosen it for him.

Rhonda was just leaving as I walked into our office.

"Did you have fun this morning?" she asked.

"Yes. It's exciting to see all the Christmas decorations downtown. I was even able to get a few stocking stuffers."

"I said I'd meet Nell and Tina for afternoon tea. Angela is hoping to join me," said Rhonda.

"Go. Have fun. I'll see you tomorrow. Annette is handling the dinner tonight."

That evening, Tina, Nell, and I watched the kids in the pool at my house while Vaughn, Clint, and Nick stood talking around the barbecue as Vaughn grilled steaks. The children had already eaten, giving the adults some moments to ourselves. From a distance, I watched the interaction between Vaughn and Nick, who'd been friends for years and kidded each other. Clint was at ease with them and added to the teasing naturally. It was rewarding to see him like this, easygoing and pleasant as he'd always been. I had the feeling that a sail with the men had helped a lot and intended to ask Vaughn about it later.

"It's lovely to be here," said Tina. "I've looked forward to it for months. I haven't said much about it, but early in the year, Nick and I faced rumors of our divorce. It wasn't true, of course, but once the rumor mill starts something like that, you can't help but go through a period of doubting."

Nell turned to her. "Do you just pretend it never happened?"

"Of course not," said Tina. "Just believe in one another and communicate. I understand you've gone through something like it."

Nell frowned and nodded. "I didn't know what to think when Claudine came into the picture. She really went after Clint. I was at home, frustrated with my life. It was a combination that could have turned out to be awful."

"I understand," said Tina. "But I hear you're going to be working at the hotel doing something you love while the kids are in school."

"I've wanted to do something useful for a long time. I mean, in addition to being there for Clint and my kids."

"It's a fine line, but I'm happy for you that you've managed to work it out," said Tina. "When I'm away for a movie, I go through the same feelings of wanting to be with my kids and still wanting to do something for myself."

Nell hugged Tina and turned to me with eyes swimming with tears. "I'm grateful I can talk to you. Women helping each other, supporting one another, is important."

I faced them. "We're family, and we'll always do that. Right?"

We smiled at one another.

At dinner, I asked Clint how the sailing had gone.

He grinned and glanced at Vaughn and Nick. "Great. I'm not going to lie; it was a challenge the first time the boat heeled. I had to remember I wasn't going to end up in the water like last time. But Vaughn knows I love sailing, and I love his boat. Once I knew I could totally relax, I was fine."

Vaughn gave him a steady look. "You're a true sailor. If you were scared, you never showed it. We've had many hours together on that boat. Now, we'll have many more."

"I understand the Coast Guard rescued you," said Tina.

"Guess why they were out there," said Vaughn. "Chasing smugglers."

"Thank God, they stopped to help," said Nell.

Clint returned her smile with such a sexy look I knew everything was right between them.

After everyone was down for the night, Vaughn and I cuddled together in our bed. I loved these times of lying close and talking.

"How did it go on the boat with Clint? I know he feels better about sailing. Did it take away some of your guilt to see him comfortable there?"

"Yeah, I guess. He had a chance to ask me some questions about what is going on for me, and I got the sense that feelings were back to normal between us."

"Oh, that makes me happy. What a relief. Tomorrow is going to be busy with our Christmas Eve dinner here at the house. Stephanie and Randolph Willis are thrilled to join us, along with Annette and Bernie. Tina, Nick, and the kids will be with us for the meal. After dinner, we'll all go to Rhonda's for dessert and a nightcap, giving the kids a chance to be together. Barring any problems at the hotel, I'll be busy here at home most of the day with a few quick runs to and from the hotel."

"I'll take the kids to do some shopping of their own and out to lunch or go wherever they want," said Vaughn. "How about that?"

I hugged him hard. "That'll be perfect."

His lips met mine, and I thought our relationship was the best gift I'd ever been given.

CHAPTER TWENTY-EIGHT

THE NEXT MORNING, CLINT ANNOUNCED THAT HE NEEDED to do some shopping. Nell told us she'd promised to go into the hotel to help. Vaughn offered to take all three children Christmas shopping, and I called Bernie to see if there were any issues at the hotel.

After telling me that everything was running smoothly, I asked Bernie to call me if necessary and said I'd see him and Annette tonight at my house for dinner. Even though he and Annette would either work at the hotel or be on call both Christmas Eve and Christmas Day, they usually took a couple of hours to attend an early dinner at my house every Christmas Eve.

I was even more excited to host my dinner this year with both Nell and Tina and their families present.

Working at a hotel with excellent food was a true benefit. Though I would prepare everything else, I would have the hotel kitchen prepare Beef Wellingtons for me to cook at home. Fortunately, there wasn't a vegetarian or vegan in the group.

Dressing the dinner tables was the most fun for me. I wrote place cards for each person—all twelve adults and nine children. Each place would have a holiday popper with a paper hat inside sitting on top of a plate. This was a tradition that had started when Robbie was still a toddler.

My cell phone rang. *Rhonda.*

"How's it going over at your house?" I asked her.

"Terrific. I've been making the desserts, and then I'll get

to work on a revised Feast of the Seven Fishes. I no longer pretend to do it exactly as I knew when I was growing up, but we'll feature a variety of fish as appetizers. Other than that, I'll make my mother's lasagna recipe and serve my wedding soup."

"Sounds yummy. I talked to Bernie. He said everything is running smoothly at the hotel. He and Annette are coming here for dinner. It's nice that you've invited Dorothy and Lorraine to your place. What can I bring to your dessert party? I've already ordered a Chantilly cake from our favorite place."

"That will be more than enough. I've made Panna Cotta, honey balls, and my chocolate torte. All traditional Italian desserts."

"Are you sure you don't want me to taste-test?" I kidded.

"I'm sure," she said, laughing. "Willow and Drew are doing an outstanding job of that."

"Have fun today. It's pleasant to enjoy the holiday away from the hotel. I've offered to help place the gifts guests ordered outside their doors if needed. But I'm really hoping they won't need me."

"They should be fine. Let's enjoy a family day," said Rhonda. "It happens very rarely for us."

"Okay," I said. "Let me know if I can bring anything else besides the cake and the chocolates I usually order from San Francisco."

"Will do," said Rhonda. "Thanks."

I ended the call.

At the table for adults, I placed my best crystal and sparkling silverware. In each dark green linen napkin, I tucked a gold-foil-wrapped chocolate truffle. While the adult table was elegant with special Lenox Holiday chinaware, the kids' table was much more fun, with melamine dinnerware displaying snowman designs. Each of their plates had a party popper on top.

Gazing around the room, I was filled with excitement. It looked festive. I could almost imagine the people sitting there, the sound of music in the background, and the buzz of conversation.

I reviewed my meal. In addition to the Beef Wellingtons, I was serving a carrot and onion casserole, which was a favorite of Vaughn's, Julia Child's potatoes au gratin, and a simple recipe of green beans and bacon that Robbie liked. To accompany the meal, I'd serve a tossed green leaf lettuce and cranberry salad.

Liz was bringing her famous toasted cheese crisps for an appetizer, and I'd supply holiday nuts. Tina and Nick were bringing wine. Stephanie and Randolph were bringing homemade lemonade for the kids. Bernie and Annette were asked not to bring anything, but they would probably bring wine.

Anticipation filled me as I checked the living room. There was seating and space for everyone, even with the large Christmas tree in the corner.

Later, I was finishing with the prep for the carrot casserole when Vaughn and the kids returned home after seeing a movie. They were wound up about the gifts they'd bought for one another. Nell had promised to help wrap those that needed it.

"I got Mommy and Daddy a big surprise," said Ned proudly, holding out a package for me to see, already wrapped by the store.

"That's very thoughtful. You'd better place it under the tree for tomorrow," I said.

"I got a present for Mom and one for Dad," said Bailey. "I'll put mine there."

I glanced at Robbie.

"I already bought gifts earlier," said Robbie. "They're already under the tree. But I bought one today for Brett. He's going to really like it."

"That's what makes it fun," I said.

A short while later, Clint returned to the house without any packages. He didn't mention doing any shopping and announced he was taking a nap.

Nell arrived in time to escort the children out of the pool and assist them in getting dressed in their special Christmas clothes.

I went to the kitchen to take care of the beef, then, as excited as the kids, I went to my bedroom to change into something festive.

Vaughn saw me enter the room and came over to me. He pulled me into a warm embrace. "Merry Christmas, darling. In all the confusion in the next couple of days, I might not get the chance to thank you for all you've done to make this holiday fun for everyone."

He put his arms around me and lowered his lips to mine. I leaned against him, feeling an overwhelming sense of gratitude for having him in my life.

Just before our guests were due to arrive, I asked Bailey to be the official door greeter. In a green velvet dress and with a green ribbon in her hair, she looked adorable.

Ned, wearing khaki pants and a red and green plaid shirt, kept running to the window to see if the Ts had arrived.

Robbie was helping Vaughn, who was setting up a bar in the butler's pantry.

Stephanie and Randolph arrived at the same time as Liz and Chad, along with their kids. They helped lead the Ts to our front door, where Bailey was calling out to them.

Chad followed, carrying Gabe in his arms, walking beside Liz, who held a tray of appetizers.

Tina, Nick, and their boys arrived next. I knew Bernie and Annette would be the last to arrive and the first to leave. It was always that way because of their duties at the hotel.

Sure enough, as dinner was about to be served, Bernie and Annette arrived. Bernie, bless his heart, was wearing a Christmas tie. Annette, who always looked elegant, was wearing a black dress with a sparkly Christmas tree pin that held real gems.

After hugs and kisses and greetings were exchanged with them, we all settled at the tables for dinner. Robbie was being a sport about being the oldest at the children's table, though Liz had promised to eventually exchange places with him to help keep the kids eating.

Before carving and doling out slices of the Beef Wellington, Vaughn stood and lifted his wine glass.

"Here's to another year of blessings. Ann and I are extremely pleased to share this meal with you because each of you is an important member of our family. Here's to another good year."

A chorus of answers followed, and then he sat down, keeping his eyes on me.

My lips curved at the sexy way he stared at me before we all popped open our poppers.

The children laughed to see everyone wearing silly hats on their heads. I loved the idea of adults playing along with the kids.

Vaughn carved the meat as dishes were passed around the adult table and servings doled out to the children. Nell had cooked chicken fingers to add to the kids' plates, keeping everyone eating.

Even though the children were seated at a separate table, they occasionally joined us adults, coming in for a snuggle or to whisper secrets. It was sweet to have them here, making Christmas memories.

The quiet hum of contented voices was like music to my ears. A scene like this, our dining room filled with friends and family, was in stark contrast to my childhood, and I treasure these moments.

As the meal was ending, Clint surprised us by getting to his feet. He looked around the table and said, "I want to thank everyone in this room for being so understanding, kind, and supportive to me and my family during these last several weeks. I especially want to thank my wife, Nell, for everything she has done for me. Because you all are special to us, I thought it only right to share this moment with you."

He pulled out a velvet-covered box from his pants pocket, walked over to Nell's chair, and knelt beside it. "Nell, I love you more than anything. I always want you by my side. Will you marry me again?"

He opened the box, showing her an eternity ring of sparkling diamonds set in platinum to match her engagement and wedding rings.

Nell stared in shock at the ring, then at him, and burst into tears. "Oh, Clint! That's the sweetest thing ever! Yes, I'll marry you again. I love you more than you know."

She stood, and he wrapped his "good" arm around her and kissed her.

Sighing with happiness and trying to control her emotions, she laid her head against his shoulder.

"I know that whatever it is, I love you more. Right, kids?" Clint turned to them, and I realized he'd planned this with them.

Bailey and Ned ran over to their parents.

"A wedding. Can I be a bridesmaid?" asked Bailey, smiling at her mother.

"Do I have to get dressed up?" Ned asked.

Laughing, the four of them hugged each other.

Vaughn began to clap, and we all joined in. As I watched this couple come together like this, I wasn't the only person in the room crying.

CHAPTER TWENTY-NINE

OUR DINNER GROUP LEFT OUR HOUSE AND WENT TO Rhonda's house in separate cars to enjoy dessert together. Another tradition that started a few years ago.

Nell was the star of the evening as she eagerly showed off her new ring and announced that she and Clint would have a second wedding at the hotel.

A crowd gathered around her.

"Let's have a gander at those big diamonds," said Rhonda, hugging Nell. "So, when's the wedding?"

"I hope it's after high season at the hotel," teased Annette.

"And after tax season," said Reggie. He and Will had followed through and offered Clint a place at their firm.

Standing arm in arm, Nell and Clint laughed as they were embraced by those who hadn't already done so.

"Come see what we have for dessert," said Rhonda. "Coffee, tea, water, and drinks are in the kitchen. The treats are in the dining room."

I'd just placed a slice of chocolate torte on my plate when Bernie's cell phone rang nearby. I watched him as he listened to whomever was speaking. His expression became more and more worried.

"What is it?" I asked.

"Part of the condo building next to the hotel is on fire. They believe it started with Christmas decorations. I've got to go."

Rhonda came over to us. "What's going on?"

While Bernie explained it to her, I found Vaughn to tell

him what had happened and that I was leaving with Bernie and Rhonda. "I'll be in touch. I'm taking my car."

"Be safe. Keep the hotel property safe," said Vaughn.

I slipped away to avoid ruining Rhonda and Will's party. Rhonda joined me at the door.

"Bernie's already left. I'll come with you," she said, looking worried.

The drive to the hotel, which takes minutes, seemed like hours. Fires could be uncontrollable if not caught early.

"God, Annie, I'd hate for the hotel to be ruined because of this. Let's pray the firemen got there on time."

"Bernie said they think the cause was Christmas decorations. Do you know what I'm thinking?"

"Oh, Gawd, Brock Goodwin was selling his decorations up and down the coastline. Do you think?" Rhonda's voice trailed off in horror.

"We don't have the facts, but even the thought of it makes me sick," I said.

Fire engines blocked the street in front of the hotel and on either side of the condo building. No flames could be seen. I parked my car inside the hotel's gates, and Rhonda and I rushed to where a group of firefighters stood outside the building. Bernie waved us over.

"What's happening?" I asked.

"The fire started on the sixth floor in one of the condos," said Bernie. "It sustained fire, smoke, and some water damage. The two apartments on either side have been affected, but the fire is contained. Thank God. It could have been a huge disaster."

I stared up at the building and at the frightened faces of the people who had been evacuated, whispering a silent prayer of thanks that no one was hurt and the fire was quickly contained.

Rhonda put her arm around me. "Having this fire

controlled this early might be the best Christmas present we could be given, don'tcha think?"

"Absolutely," I said, spotting Brock in the crowd. There was a part of me that wanted to know if he was somehow involved, but I turned away. I didn't want anything to rip apart the gratitude I felt for the safety of the people who lived there.

Bernie looked at each of us. "Why don't you go back to your families? There's really nothing for you to do here."

"Thanks," I said. "We'll check in at the hotel, and if everyone is fine there, we'll go home, leaving them in your capable hands." I gave him a quick embrace. "Thank you. And Merry Christmas."

"Yes, Bernie, Merry Christmas. We'll see you tomorrow," said Rhonda.

We walked back to the hotel. A crowd of hotel guests had gathered in the lobby.

"What's going on?" several asked.

Rhonda and I explained what had happened and hoped that the disturbance next door with the firetrucks hadn't frightened them.

A couple of children were in the group, dressed in pajamas. They'd obviously been awakened by the commotion.

I knelt in front of one little boy. "Everything is fine. Are you excited about Christmas?"

He grinned. "Mommy and Daddy told Santa Claus we'd be at The Beach House Hotel."

"Well, then, guess you'd better go to sleep so you can wake up to Christmas."

His mother beamed at me. "Thanks for your assurance. Everyone here at the hotel has been very kind and understanding. Spending Christmas here is always special."

"Enjoy," said Rhonda. She turned to the group of people walking away, "Merry Christmas, everyone!"

The employee at the front desk gave us a thumbs up, and

then Rhonda and I walked away.

Outside, I stopped and stared at the front of the elegant hotel.

"She's a beauty," said Rhonda.

"Truly."

Taking another moment, I gazed at the palm fronds caressing the night air with the help of the sea breezes coming onto the shore. They added to the hotel's beauty.

" 'C'mon," said Rhonda. "We'd better get back to our families."

At Rhonda's house, the party was still going. I gazed at the group of friends, thankful once more that everyone here was safe and looking forward to the celebration.

The kids were beginning to fuss, and seeing the fatigue on Liz's face, I went to her. "How about my helping you get the kids settled for the night? Chad needs his freedom to spend with the other men."

"Oh, Mom, that would be great. They're on a sugar high and beyond excited. Getting them into bed and asleep won't be easy. Do you remember how you used to sing to me? Maybe you can do that."

I chuckled. I had no singing voice, but she'd always loved bedtime songs.

We said goodbye to everyone, and I helped walk the Ts to the car and climbed into the van with them.

Liz drove to her house, parked, and together we got the children inside, washed up, and into their pajamas. Gabe, the youngest, was half asleep when we put him in his crib. But the Ts were not about to succumb quietly.

Noah joined his sisters in their room and lay tucked under the cover on Olivia's bed.

Seeing their eager expressions waiting for me to begin, my eyes stung with tears. Liz had been afraid of never having children. And now she had four.

"Gammy, sing Rudolph," said Emily.

I started singing it in a low voice so I wouldn't disturb Gabe.

"Now, Frosty," said Noah.

It took another six songs, each one softer, to make their eyelids droop and their breathing slow. I didn't realize Liz was watching from the doorway and Chad had joined her until I heard their quiet "thank you".

Chad walked into the bedroom and lifted Noah in his arms to carry him to his bed. Though Noah mumbled something, he remained asleep.

"I'll take you home," said Liz. "It'll give me a chance to talk to Nell. I'm ecstatic about the news of a wedding vow renewal."

"Me, too," I said with feeling.

I hugged Chad goodbye, and we left for my house.

When we entered the house, I immediately noticed that the people we'd paid to clean up from dinner had done their job. Relieved, Nell and I joined the others.

Nell and Clint were sitting in the living room with Vaughn.

"Hi," Nell said. "Bailey and Ned are finally asleep. We're just relaxing here."

"I want to tell you and Clint how very proud I am of you," I said, facing them as they sat on the couch. "A vow renewal is a beautiful way to recommit to a relationship. It's a lovely thing for you to do, Clint."

He grinned. "I like the idea."

"Let me see the ring again," said Liz. "When is the wedding going to take place?"

Nell glanced at Clint. "I've always wanted to get married

in April. It didn't work out last time. But now we can do it and have a true April in Paris second honeymoon."

Clint grinned. "Sounds fine to me as long as it's toward the end of the month, after Tax Day on the fifteenth."

Nell leaned over and kissed him. "Perfect." She stood. "C'mon, Liz. Let's go chat."

The girls left, and Clint said, "Guess I'd better put together a couple of toys for the kids."

"I'll help," said Vaughn.

"I'll check on Robbie," I said.

When I looked in on Robbie, I found him lying on top of his bed. Cindy was asleep, nestled up against him as he played some games on his phone.

"Ready to settle down for the night? Bailey and Ned will get up very early to awaken us." I sat on the edge of his bed. "Did you have a pleasant day?"

He nodded. "Stephanie and Randolph will be here tomorrow morning, right?"

"Yes," I said. "They wouldn't miss it for the world."

"I have a special present for each of them because they're my grandparents. Right?"

"Yes, your grandparents of our hearts," I said. "We were lucky to find them."

"I like it," said Robbie. " 'Night, Mom."

"I love you, son." I kissed him and patted Cindy, pleased that my house was full.

When I went into the bedroom, I found Vaughn waiting in bed for me.

After I got ready for the night, I joined him.

He pulled me to him and kissed me. "Merry Christmas, Ann. Another good year."

"For me, too," I said, resting my head on his chest. "And a better year to come."

CHAPTER THIRTY

THE FOUR MONTHS FOLLOWING CHRISTMAS FLEW BY IN A flurry of hotel activity. With each passing day, we became more focused on Nell and Clint's upcoming event. They'd chosen Saturday, April 24th, as their wedding day.

Rhonda and I were walking on the beach a few days before Ty and his family were due to arrive for the ceremony.

She turned to me. "Ya know, Annie, it's sweet to see you this excited about Nell's wedding. It doesn't seem that long ago that you were worried about her and her marriage. I think I'm as proud of Nell as you are. Our three daughters building a life together makes me feel very confident about the future of The Beach House Hotel."

"They're bright, smart, and hard-working women. More than that, they're supportive of one another," I said, feeling the same way about the future.

"I'm not quite ready to retire, but it's comforting to know that when the time is right for the two of us to step back, we'll have our girls ready to take over," said Rhonda.

"I'm pleased that Nell is part of it. I love having her here in Sabal at last."

"Uh-oh," said Rhonda, her whole demeanor changing. "Guess what slimy, lying, pest is approaching."

I turned to see Brock walking toward us, bouncing on his feet as he approached with a swagger.

" 'Morning, ladies," he said with a smile that didn't reach his eyes. "Guess you heard, the fire department has cleared me and my company of any responsibility for that condo fire on Christmas Eve."

I studied him, trying to figure out why Brock was such a snake. He was a handsome man, but an unpleasant person. "What I heard is that Christmas lights were at fault, with a concern about the flammability of the decorations."

"Guess you won't be selling more of those," said Rhonda.

"I've got something even better. I just brought in a line of decorative pottery from Italy. It's something I thought you might be interested in for the hotel," he said. "I can give you a deal."

"Not on your fuckin' life," mumbled Rhonda.

Brock shook his head. "Aw, that's not neighborly, Rhonda. Can't we be friends?"

"I don't believe you know what the word means," I said. "Let's just go our separate ways."

He blocked my departure. "You know, as president of the Neighborhood Association, I can make your lives miserable."

"You already do," Rhonda said. "So, what's the threat in that?"

Brock glared at Rhonda. "If you try to interfere with my business, I'll get you for it."

"Oh, my! Is that a threat?" asked Rhonda.

I took hold of Rhonda's elbow and led her away from Brock before Rhonda completely lost her temper.

"That man makes me so damn mad," said Rhonda. She looked back to make sure he wasn't following us. "I know he was behind the recent story exposing certain guests hiding out at the hotel."

"No doubt about it," I agreed. "But the one thing his ego doesn't like is us ignoring him. Let's go inside. I hear Consuela is making her chocolate chip cookies."

"Well, then, let's hurry," said Rhonda, winking at me.

I laughed, and we headed inside.

The next day, Vaughn and I waited at the airport to pick up Ty, June, and their kids, seven-year-old Bo and his five-year-old sister, Rosie. We saw them as often as possible, but with them living on the West Coast, outside of San Francisco, it could be difficult. Vaughn's schedule allowed him to visit more often than I could manage, but that didn't mean I was any less excited to see them.

We waited at the appropriate place inside the terminal. When I saw them walking toward us, I waved frantically and waited for the kids to run to greet me.

"Hi, Gammie," cried Rosie, lifting her arms to me. She was small for her age with a gracefulness that came from her mother.

I picked her up and twirled her around. "How's one of my favorite girls?"

"I'm here, but it took forever," said Rosie, staring at me with dark brown eyes. I set her down to allow her to greet Vaughn, and turned to Bo to give him a big hug. The children were beautiful and very well-behaved. Their mother, June, was loving but strict, with oversight from her mother and her aunties, who adored the kids. Having never been part of a normal family, I was a bit overwhelmed when I first met her parents and all her relatives.

While Vaughn and Ty exchanged hugs, I kissed June hello. "I'm thrilled we get to have you here for a few days alone before the wedding. We don't see you often enough."

"Thanks," she said, hugging me. "We're looking forward to relaxing here. And to help celebrate Nell's wedding, of course."

I hugged Ty, and then we all walked to the baggage claim area. I knew from the smile on Vaughn's face that he was as pleased as I was to start the week off this way.

On our way home, both Nell and Liz called June to see if they'd arrived. My heart was happy to hear the girls' chatter. I thought how lucky they were to be this compatible.

After things were settled at the house, Bo and Rosie wanted to go into the pool. Although the air felt cool to me, for visitors from different areas, the temperature was perfect. Besides, our pool was heated.

The kids had just jumped into the water when Nell arrived with Bailey and Ned. The four played in the pool while the adults sat around and watched them.

Ty and Nell were siblings who obviously loved one another. Ty had his father's dark hair and eyes, while Nell resembled her mother with blond hair and blue eyes. However, there was a similarity in the way they spoke and moved that was reminiscent of Vaughn.

Nell and June left us to go inside for girl talk.

Liz arrived a short while later with her four children, dressed for the pool.

The Ts had no problem mixing in with the other kids. I made sure to give Gabe, who was the youngest, my attention. He was adorable with strawberry-blond hair like Chad.

Holding him in my lap for a snuggle, I watched the kids playing and let out a long, grateful sigh. I'd felt hopeless trying for more children after Liz, never dreaming I'd be this blessed with grandchildren.

The next few days were filled with all kinds of activities. Ty and Vaughn were able to get away for a private sail on Vaughn's boat, and then Vaughn and Ty were joined by Clint and Reggie. Clint was a sport about the teasing he took about ducking out of the way of the boom while the boat was coming about.

The girls shopped, gossiped, and hung together as much as possible while Rhonda and I helped by watching over the children, with Liana and her friend's help.

The wedding was going to be small, with just my family members, Rhonda and her entire family, Stephanie and Randolph, Bernie and Annette, Lorraine, and Lauren from the hospitality department, making a total of twenty-some people. The timing was perfect for everyone to be present, as it coincided with spring break from school.

Clint and Nell had decided that this ceremony would be all about the children. Bailey was scheduled to be the maid of honor, and Ned was the best man.

Nell asked her father if he'd be disappointed if she had Robbie, the oldest of the children, walk her onto the beach. Vaughn gracefully said no.

On the day of the wedding, Rhonda hosted a luncheon at Andre's for all the women who were attending the ceremony, declaring it a rare opportunity to have this occasion together.

All of us dressed up for the affair, and as I looked around the small, private dining room, admiring gleaming new manicures and styled hair, I was glad to be part of this festive occasion. Now that the high season was over at the hotel, it was important for us women to be able to celebrate as a group.

As soon as everyone was seated and champagne served, Rhonda got to her feet.

"It's fabulous to see all my favorite women gathered here today to celebrate Nell's wedding later this afternoon. I feel very honored to have you here. Here's to a lovely wedding, Nell!"

"Hear! Hear!" we all cried.

I stood. "I want to say how proud I am of Nell. She's an example of a strong woman working to make life right for herself and her family."

After I sat down, Nell stood and raised her tulip glass of

champagne. "I want to thank you all for being here for me. I needed to make changes in my life, but it wasn't until I came to Sabal and received your support that I was able to do it."

We raised our glasses to her and then took a sip.

"Okay, now that we've got that taken care of, let's eat," said Rhonda as the waitresses carried in our lunches: asparagus quiches and leafy green salads.

"This is the healthy part," announced Rhonda. "I've saved the best for last. Wait until you see our desserts."

I laughed with the others. This was a sweet beginning to the celebration that was about to happen.

CHAPTER THIRTY-ONE

IN THE LATE AFTERNOON, I DRESSED FOR THE BEACH wedding in a flowing floral skirt and a pink silk blouse. Nell and Clint had requested that we all dress casually. The men would no doubt follow Clint's choice of khaki pants and polo shirts. I knew Liz and June were wearing sundresses, and I was certain most of the others would wear pretty spring skirts or dresses as well.

Bo and Rosie were beside themselves with excitement. They'd spent the whole week playing with their cousins and were excited to be included in a wedding. Bailey had told them and the other kids about her important role. Ned wasn't as excited, but I knew he would be when the moment came.

I left my bedroom and went to see what I could do to help Robbie. He looked very grown-up in his khaki pants and a blue polo shirt, with his dark hair slicked back.

"Are you ready to help Clint?" I asked him.

"I told him I'd meet him at the hotel," said Robbie with a note of pride.

I checked my watch. "I guess we'd better go. Where's Dad?"

"Outside talking to Ty," he said.

We left his room and found everyone gathered outside, dressed for the wedding.

"Robbie and I want to go to the hotel to help Nell and Clint," I said. "You've got a little more time."

"I'll come with you," said Vaughn. "Ty, you can take my car. Okay?"

"Sure, Dad. We'll follow in a little bit."

As Vaughn drove to the hotel, I could see the tension in his shoulders. I knew this was a big moment for him, even though Robbie would be walking Nell onto the beach.

"How are you doing?" I asked him as Robbie turned on his earphones.

"It may be the second time around for Nell and Clint, but in some ways, it feels like the first one," he said. "I'm proud of them."

"You're not feeling left out, are you?" I asked.

"No, I'm very proud that my son, Robbie, is going to walk Nell onto the beach. But I'll still be the one giving her away all over again, as Nell put it."

I loved the tender look that crossed his face.

We arrived at the hotel, and I immediately went to the bridal suite where Nell, Angie, Liz, and June were gathering. The children would be part of the ceremony, but the real essence of the wedding was the behind-the-scenes support.

When I saw Nell in her wedding gown —a pale pink silk midi dress with capped sleeves and a sweetheart neckline — my breath caught. She was stunning. Her blond hair was pulled away from her face in a type of braid, into which a few orchids had been placed.

"Oh, my darling, you are beautiful," I whispered as I hugged her.

"Thank you for helping me pick out the dress," she said. She looked around the room. "Ready, everybody?"

"I know how excited you are, but give us time to get onto the beach," said Liz with a teasing smile.

Robbie knocked on the door.

I let him in and then we women left.

Standing on the beach between Vaughn and Liz, I listened to the guitar music, felt the gentle sea breezes brush my cheeks, and let out a joyful sigh. This was such a special occasion. The situation between Nell and Clint could've ended very differently.

The lapping of the nearby water made a soothing sound. It blended with the classical guitar music being played. I gazed at the small, white wooden altar that had been placed in the sand. A huge arrangement of pink flowers, including roses and orchids, sat in a white wicker basket atop the altar with electric candles flanking it.

The woman overseeing the ceremony was a friend of ours who officiated at weddings all over the area.

Ned proudly stood by his father near the altar that had been placed in a quiet section of the beach in front of the hotel. Seeing him like this, I could well imagine Ned as a grown adult.

The circle of people of all ages waited in anticipation. Even the children, as excited as they were, behaved.

When the guitar player shifted to a new song, John Legend's *All of Me*, I turned and watched as Bailey, in a pink halter dress and wearing a crown of orchids to match her mother's, stepped onto the sand, a darling maid of honor.

Smiling, she held onto a bouquet of pink flowers that matched the arrangement on the altar, and bravely made her barefoot way to her father.

When she was in place opposite Ned and their father, the guitar music switched to *Perfect* by Ed Sheeran.

We turned to see Nell.

Robbie held onto his sister's arm, carefully leading Nell onto the beach.

Gasps of delight echoed around me as Nell, smiling, walked toward us, but she had eyes only for Clint.

Watching her, Clint's eyes welled up with tears. Bailey

and Ned looked as proud of their mother as I felt. Vaughn squeezed my hand, and I knew he was feeling emotional like the rest of us. Seeing a couple get married for the first time was special, filled with hopes for a happy future that were shared by all.

But this evening, with the sun lowering in the sky and the sea breezes whispering endearments, this wedding couldn't be matched because we all knew what it had taken to reach this point.

I glanced at Rhonda. She and I had hosted many weddings at The Beach House Hotel and would continue to do so. Moments like this made all our hard work worth it, allowing us to provide such a lovely setting. We shared the hopes and dreams of all who came here to be joined in matrimony and welcomed those who came for rest, privacy, fun, and excellent food.

Standing on the opposite side of the circle, wiping her tears, Rhonda winked at me. I knew she was as proud as I was that we'd accomplished what we'd set out to do. On a sea breeze, I blew her a kiss, and she sent one back.

# # # # #

Thank you for reading *Sea Breezes at The Beach House Hotel*. If you enjoyed this book, please help other readers discover it by leaving a review on Amazon, Bookbub, Goodreads, or your favorite site. It's such a nice thing to do.

For your further enjoyment the other books in The Beach House Hotel Series are available on all sites. Here are the Universal links:

Breakfast at The Beach House Hotel:
https://books2read.com/u/bpkoq4

Lunch at The Beach House Hotel:
https://books2read.com/u/3GWvp3

Dinner at The Beach House Hotel:
https://books2read.com/u/4N1yDW

Christmas at The Beach House Hotel:
https://books2read.com/u/38gZvd

Margaritas at The Beach House Hotel:
https://books2read.com/u/bMRrP7

Dessert at The Beach House Hotel:
https://books2read.com/u/mV6kX6

Coffee at The Beach House Hotel:
https://books2read.com/u/bOnE7A

High Tea at The Beach House Hotel:
https://books2read.com/u/mgN9AK

Nightcaps at The Beach House Hotel:
https://books2read.com/u/mBA2oy

Bubbles at The Beach House Hotel:

https://books2read.com/u/meGgRV

Sign up for my newsletter and get a free story. I keep my newsletters short and fun with giveaways, recipes, and the latest must-have news about me and my books. Welcome! Here's the link:

https://BookHip.com/RRGJKGN

About the Author

A *USA Today* **Best-Selling Author,** Judith Keim is a hybrid author who both has a publisher and self-publishes. Ms. Keim writes heart-warming novels about women who face unexpected challenges, meet them with strength, and find love and happiness along the way—stories with heart. Her best-selling books are based, in part, on many of the places she's lived or visited and on the interesting people she's met, creating believable characters and realistic settings her many loyal readers love.

She enjoyed her childhood and young adult years in Elmira, New York, and now makes her home in Boise, Idaho, with her husband, Peter, and their lovable miniature Dachshunds, Wally and Kacy, and other members of her family.

While growing up, she was drawn to the idea of writing stories from a young age. Books were always present, being read, ready to go back to the library, or about to be discovered. All in her family shared information in general conversation, giving them a wealth of knowledge and vivid imaginations.

Ms. Keim loves to hear from her readers and appreciates their enthusiasm for her stories.

"I hope you've enjoyed this book. If you have, please help

other readers discover it by leaving a review on the site of your choice. And please check out my other books and series:

The Hartwell Women Series
The Beach House Hotel Series
The Fat Fridays Group
The Salty Key Inn Series
The Chandler Hill Inn Series
Seashell Cottage Books
The Desert Sage Inn Series
Soul Sisters at Cedar Mountain Lodge
The Sanderling Cove Inn Series
The Lilac Lake Inn Series
Lilac Lake Books

"ALL THE BOOKS ARE NOW AVAILABLE IN AUDIO on Audible, iTunes, Findaway, Kobo, and Google Play! So fun to have these characters come alive!"

Ms. Keim can be reached at **www.judithkeim.com**

"To like my author page on Facebook and keep up with the news, go to: **http://bit.ly/2pZWDgA**

"To receive notices about new books, follow me on Book Bub: **https://www.bookbub.com/authors/judith-keim**

"Sign up for my newsletter and get a free story. I keep my newsletters short and fun with giveaways, recipes, and the latest must-have news about me and my books. Welcome! Here's the link:
https://BookHip.com/RRGJKGN

"I am also on Twitter @judithkeim, LinkedIn, and Goodreads. Come say hello!"

Acknowledgments

As always, I am eternally grateful to my team of editors, Peter Keim and Lynn Mapp, my book cover designer, May Dawney, and my narrator for Audible and iTunes, Angela Dawe. They are the people who take what I've written and help turn it into the book I proudly present to you, my readers! I also wish to thank my coffee group of writers who listen and encourage me to keep on going. Thank you, Peggy Staggs, Lynn Mapp, Cate Cobb, Nikki Jean Triska, Joanne Pence, Melanie Olsen, and Megan Bryce. And to you, my fabulous readers, I thank you for your continued support and encouragement. Without you, this book would not exist. You are the wind beneath my wings.

www.ingramcontent.com/pod-product-compliance
Lightning Source LLC
LaVergne TN
LVHW040046080526
838202LV00045B/3507